W

VIRTUAL DIG

Second Edition

A Simulated Archaeological Excavation of a Middle Paleolithic Site in France

Harold L. Dibble
University of Pennsylvania

Shannon P. McPherron
University of North Carolina at Greensboro

Barbara J. Roth
University of Nevada, Las Vegas

Program by:

Shannon P. McPherron

Workbook by:

Barbara J. Roth

Harold L. Dibble

 **McGraw-Hill**
Mayfield

Boston   Burr Ridge, IL   Dubuque, IA   Madison, WI   New York   San Francisco   St. Louis
Bangkok   Bogotá   Caracas   Kuala Lumpur   Lisbon   London   Madrid   Mexico City
Milan   Montreal   New Delhi   Santiago   Seoul   Singapore   Sydney   Taipei   Toronto

McGraw-Hill Higher Education
A Division of The **McGraw-Hill** Companies

ISBN-13: 978-0-07-254953-9
ISBN-10: 0-07-254953-X

567890 BKM BKM 098

Sponsoring editor, Kevin Witt; *production editor,* Jennifer Chambliss; *manuscript editor,* Amy Marks; *design manager,* Sharon Spurlock; *cover designer,* Sharon Spurlock; *art editor,* Emma Ghiselli; *production supervisor,* Pam Augspurger. This text was set in 10½/13 Berthold Baskerville by TBH Typecast, Inc. and printed on acid-free, 50# Williamsburg Offset by Quebecor Dubuque.

Cover and interior photos courtesy of Harold L. Dibble or Shannon P. McPherron; page 9: T. D. Price and G. M. Feinman. 1997. *Images of the Past.* Mountain View, CA: Mayfield Publishing Company; page 11: A. Debénath and H. L. Dibble. 1994. *The Handbook of Paleolithic Typology,* Vol. I. University of Pennsylvania Museum Publications, Fig. 2.3, courtesy of University of Pennsylvania Museum; pages 20, 21: H. L. Dibble and M. Lenoir, eds. 1995. *The Middle Paleolithic Site of Combe-Capelle Bas (France).* University of Pennsylvania Museum Publications, with permission from the publisher; page 85: with permission from the Bishop Museum.

www.mhhe.com

To the memories of Paul Fitte, who introduced us to the site of Combe-Capelle, and Mr. and Mme. René Denuel, who owned La Forge.

Preface

With the increased use of computer technology in the classroom today, the need for applications of computer technology to teach fieldwork has become a reality. The idea behind *Virtual Dig* is to use computers to teach students the basics of excavation methods in archaeology and also to have fun. We have designed this program so that it provides a feel for doing archaeology without the time and expense of a field school. Although it is not a complete substitute for field experience, it gives students an opportunity to address issues that are not always presented in the typical classroom situation, such as how to set up a research design, deal with the logistics of a field project, and develop a fundable budget. As such, *Virtual Dig* is more realistic than a standard text and provides opportunities to explore a wide range of situations that will be encountered in the field. The interactive nature of the program also allows students to experiment using different excavation techniques.

We have written the software and this workbook for lower division undergraduate students in an archaeology methods course and have geared it specifically toward anthropology majors. *Virtual Dig* is designed so that it can be used in conjunction with other introductory methods texts to elaborate on or cover material that is not covered in the software or workbook.

One of the major strengths of *Virtual Dig* is that it uses real data from the excavation of Combe-Capelle, a Middle Paleolithic site in the Dordogne region of southern France that we excavated in the early 1990s. The use of Combe-Capelle for teaching excavation methods has several advantages. First, we worked there and are familiar with it; this enhances the integration of the software and workbook. Second, the field and analytical data from Combe-Capelle were fully computerized and therefore were easily adapted to this format. We saw a logical progression to go from the computerized field and analysis techniques to publication of the Combe-Capelle data on CD-ROM (Dibble and McPherron 1996, 1997) to teaching about excavation using Combe-Capelle data in a computerized format.

Another advantage of using Combe-Capelle data is that it provides a case study that allows students to carry out a project from start to finish: from developing a research design, excavating the site, and doing the analysis to writing up the final report. Because they are based on real data, the results of the virtual excavations will be similar to what we obtained during the real excavation. This means that should they want to, students can compare their results with those presented in the published volume on Combe-Capelle (Dibble and Lenoir 1995). In fact, students could even make new discoveries about the Paleolithic.

There are some disadvantages to using Combe-Capelle as a case study, but we feel these are more than compensated for by the advantages. First, Combe-Capelle is a Paleolithic site and as such lacks things like features, bones, burials, and tombs that might be found at other archaeological sites. Second, Paleolithic techniques are somewhat specialized and adhere to specific traditions that often differ from techniques more common in North American archaeology. However, the basics of archaeology are the same whether they are done at a Paleolithic site or a Maya tomb, and the use of a Paleolithic site, with its focus on lithic typology and technology, should thus be seen as an example of the ways archaeologists use archaeological data.

TECHNICAL SUPPORT

If you experience a problem with the program that you cannot resolve, or if you need customer support, please call 1-800-331-5094 between 9 A.M. and 5 P.M. EST. Before contacting customer support, please have the following information available:

- A description of what you did and what happened
- The version of *Virtual Dig* you are using
- A description of the computer you are using and its operating system
- An exact description of any error message

Our support staff will address your problem as quickly as possible.

ACKNOWLEDGMENTS

We wish to thank a number of people who have been instrumental in seeing *Virtual Dig* become a reality. Mr. A. Bruce Mainwaring supported the initial development of this project and was a constant and eager supporter. Thanks go to Mayfield/McGraw-Hill, specifically Jan Beatty and Jennifer Chambliss; Jeremy Sabloff, Vince Pigott, and the University of Pennsylvania Museum; the Bishop Museum; Oregon State University; and Greg Farrington at the Moore School of Engineering, University of Pennsylvania. Thanks also go to Brad Evans, Phil Chase, April Nowell, Anna Agbe-Davis, and the General Honors I class at the University of Pennsylvania for their helpful comments and suggestions. A grant from the National Science Foundation (BNS 8804379) supported the bulk of the excavation costs at Combe-Capelle. We would also like to thank our reviewers: George Gumerman IV, Northern Arizona University, and his fall 1998 Anthropology 101 class; Sarah K. Campbell, Western Washington University; Mark Hartmann, University of Arkansas; and John P. Staeck, College of DuPage. Last, but by no means least, we would like to thank our families for putting up with us and supporting us while we worked on this project.

Contents

PART V   ANALYSIS

Overview of *Virtual Dig*

1

Archaeologists face many challenges in setting up a field project, excavating a site, analyzing the collected data, and interpreting the results. *Virtual Dig* is designed to give you an idea of what it is like to carry out an excavation project from start to finish. This workbook and the CD-ROM take you through a project step by step, and we have divided both of them into five major parts to follow these steps: background information, field project setup, the excavation itself, lab work on the recovered material, and analysis of the data.

We have included specific exercises designed to teach concepts presented on the CD-ROM and in the workbook. For most of these exercises, you will use this book and turn in papers or projects to your instructor. *Virtual Dig* can be used in conjunction with general introductory archaeology textbooks (e.g., Hayden 1993; Sharer and Ashmore 1993; Thomas 1995) and with the published volumes on our excavations at Combe-Capelle (Dibble and Lenoir 1995; Dibble and McPherron 1996) if you would like to explore these concepts in more depth.

In addition to these exercises, you may design and carry out what we have called a virtual project. This is a semester- or quarter-long project that allows you to set up an excavation project and see it through to writing up the final report. For the virtual project, you will excavate Combe-Capelle to answer research questions that you develop. The data generated during *Virtual Dig* will be based on actual data from our excavations (see "A Word about the Data Used in *Virtual Dig*," later in this chapter), but it is up to you to excavate the site and analyze the data to answer your research questions.

Although we recommend that you do the exercises and your virtual project from beginning to end, you have a tremendous amount of flexibility in terms of how you use the program. With the aid and advice of your instructor, you may wish to explore only certain parts of the CD-ROM or develop your own course of study. Almost everything—data, graphs, images—can be printed or exported to other programs.

We have based the CD-ROM on our excavations at the Middle Paleolithic site of Combe-Capelle, located in the Couze River valley of southwestern France. We begin by giving you background information on the

Middle Paleolithic in general and on the site of Combe-Capelle in particular. This discussion is enhanced through the use of full-color images accessible on the CD-ROM.

The next step is to set up your excavation project. You will learn how to write a research design, how to define and place your excavation units, and how to decide what methods to use for excavating the site. You will also learn about selecting project personnel, planning the logistics of a field project, and developing a budget. This will culminate in writing a grant proposal and budget that you will submit to a granting agency in order to obtain the funding necessary to do the fieldwork for your virtual project. Getting money is never easy, and you will learn some of the issues that must be addressed in order to get your proposal past anonymous reviewers.

After you set up your project, you will excavate the site. *Virtual Dig* provides an interactive interface for excavating Combe-Capelle. Using interactive excavation, you will excavate the site "by hand" and learn the basics of stratigraphy, proveniencing, screening, and field documentation. In addition to giving you a basic feel for what excavation is like, we have also tried to simulate some of the unexpected events that happen during an excavation project and that ultimately affect your budget. If you choose, you can also excavate in a way that only a computer simulation could offer, fully automatic excavation, which can save you a considerable amount of time. At any time, you can instantly access the full Combe-Capelle data set generated by our excavations.

After you finish excavating, you will analyze the data you have collected. *Virtual Dig* teaches you the basics of stone tool (lithic) analysis, technology, and typology, focusing on the analysis of Paleolithic lithic assemblages. We also provide you with an overview of basic statistics and teach you how to generate tables and a variety of charts and graphs that can be used in your analysis. Finally, you will complete an exercise on evaluating site taphonomy, or the formation of an archaeological site, to see how the site of Combe-Capelle has been affected by geological processes. After you have completed the analysis for your virtual project, you will write a final report on the results of your excavations at Combe-Capelle.

While we hope this is a valuable learning experience on excavating a site, we also hope you have fun with it!

INSTALLING THE *VIRTUAL DIG* SOFTWARE

Install the *Virtual Dig* software by inserting the CD-ROM into your computer's CD-ROM drive, click on the **Start** button, then choose the **Run** option. In the space provided, type the drive letter of your CD-ROM, followed by a colon and **setup.exe** (for example, **e:setup.exe**) or choose **Browse** to find this file on the CD-ROM. During installation you will be given an opportunity to indicate where you would like the program and necessary data files to be located. The setup program will create a program group with an icon for running the **Vdig.exe** program, or you can click on **Vdig.exe** from Windows Explorer, or create your own shortcut.

Each database file you create requires approximately 4 MB of disk storage. Depending on the amount of material you excavate, the file will increase in size. You must use the same file for your virtual project throughout the time that you are working with the program or you will lose any work you have already done.

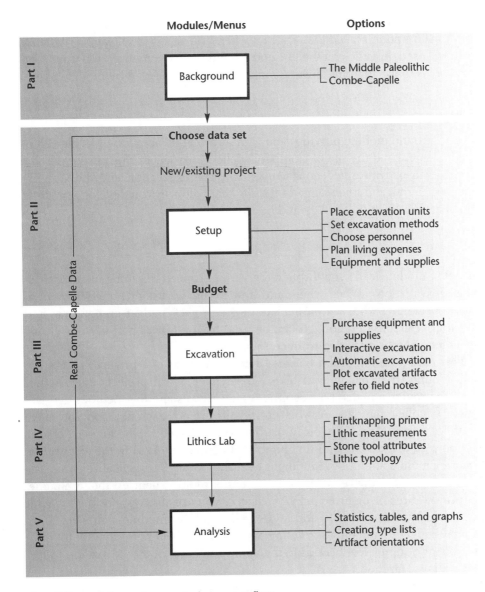

Virtual Dig modules and suggested program flow

If you want to experiment with the software, don't use your project file. You should make periodic backups of your file. For the exercises that are not based on your virtual project, you can open up as many new files as you like, delete them as you wish, or reuse them.

HOW TO USE THE *VIRTUAL DIG* SOFTWARE

Virtual Dig is organized into a series of modules that mirror the steps you take in an excavation project. These modules are reflected in the five major sections of this workbook: Background, Setup, Excavation, Lithics Lab, and Analysis. Although it makes sense to follow this order in using the software, it is not necessary to do so because each module can be used independently of the others.

You can gain access to the various modules in two ways. The easiest way is via the main option screen that appears when you start the software or when a screen is closed. Just click on the line corresponding to the module you want. The other way is to use the pull-down menus, which are organized by module name.

Background

The Background module provides you with information about the Middle Paleolithic in general and the site of Combe-Capelle in particular. The purpose of this module is to provide intellectual context for the excavation and the Combe-Capelle material, and knowledge of the site that will help you develop a realistic and efficient excavation strategy and budget.

Setup

The Setup module leads you through the various aspects of setting up an archaeological excavation project: where and how to dig, what kinds of equipment to use, the personnel who will participate in the project, budget preparation, and other logistical considerations. It can be used by itself or as part of your virtual project, or it can be excluded from consideration.

This module is important because it covers aspects of a project that are not usually found in archaeological texts. All archaeological projects must be designed to provide a match between the research goals and the methods that will be used to collect the data. As you set up your project, each decision you make will affect your budget. Obviously the budget is affected by the amount of area that you plan to excavate and the number of people involved in the excavation. Because a limited amount of funding is available for archaeological research, the idea is to maximize the return for the amount of money spent. At the same time, as a project director or principal investigator, you are also responsible for your crew's safety and comfort. To add to the realism of this module, you will submit the final budget to a fictitious granting agency, which will not only rate the proposal but also supply feedback as to the appropriateness of the excavation procedures and organization.

The planning and budget are highly integrated with the Excavation module and provide more realism to the program in terms of budgeted expenditures and crew morale. During excavation, money is spent in three ways. First, transportation, lodging, and subsistence costs are handled automatically by the software and are charged once the digging begins. Second, you must purchase equipment and supplies for the project, and these are also charged against the budget. This can be done at any time during excavation, although some purchases will be necessary before any excavation can take place. Finally, unexpected, seemingly random events occur during the course of the excavation that will often cost the project money. Although some of these events are truly random, most reflect issues related to crew morale, which is a function of how much planning went into the crew's comfort and safety.

The idea behind the integration of the budget and the excavation process is to show how money is actually spent versus it was planned to be spent. A major challenge of your virtual project is to stay within the limits of your budget. Because excavations can be run in arrears, you can spend more than you were allotted, but this will be recorded by the program, and your actual expenses can be turned in with your final site report. This means that it is possible for you to conduct an excavation project without paying attention to the budget.

Excavation

After acquiring funding, you can begin excavation. You will first choose the mode of excavation that you want to use: interactive excavation or automatic excavation. In interactive excavation mode you will remove sediment and record artifact provenience "by hand," that is, by moving your computer's mouse over the ground surface and scraping away dirt. You must also empty or screen buckets as they are filled. This is a very realistic simulation of what an excavation is like, but just like the real thing, it is slow. A faster way to dig is by using the automatic excavation mode, in which the computer does the digging and recording for you and at a much higher rate of speed. Remember, unless you are using the real data from Combe-Capelle (which has already been excavated), the only way to get material for analysis is through excavation.

Other concepts covered in the Excavation module include equipping your excavation, creating maps and plans of artifact distributions, and using field notebooks.

Lithics Lab

Because most of the material recovered from Combe-Capelle consists of lithics (stone tools and the byproducts of their manufacture), the Lithics Lab module provides you with some background on the nature of stone tool variability. There are four sections to the Lithics Lab module. The first is an interactive program to teach the fundamentals of flintknapping, from removing a flake from a core to retouching the flake into a recognizable tool. The next three sections cover lithic measurements, common stone tool attributes that are observed and recorded during lithic analysis, and lithic typology. You are first taught how to record proper measurements and recognize particular attributes or types, and then you are given a test based on a set of tools from Combe-Capelle. When coupled with the discussion presented in this workbook, these sections not only provide an introduction to the analysis of lithics (the single most common class of evidence in the archaeological record) but also prepare you to make inferences based on the analysis of data derived from your excavations at the site.

Analysis

The Analysis module has three main goals: to teach you the basics of modern lithic analysis, to develop your skills in dealing with quantitative data, and to use archaeological data to make inferences about your virtual project. Of course, analysis requires data, and the data you use in this module can come from two sources: your own excavations in *Virtual Dig* or the data acquired during our excavation at Combe-Capelle.

Three sections in the Analysis module provide you with an opportunity to work with data. The first section teaches you the difference between numeric and character data and the kinds of statistics, tables, and graphs that work best for each. You can organize your data in a number of ways and generate output either to the screen or to the printer. The other two sections are for specialized analyses.

The first deals specifically with typological data and can calculate and graph type counts, or classes of artifacts, for specified levels or units. The second does the same with orientation data and illustrates the usefulness of orientation analysis (how the artifacts are positioned in the ground) for addressing issues of site formation and disturbance.

A WORD ABOUT THE DATA USED IN *VIRTUAL DIG*

The data used in *Virtual Dig* are the actual data recovered during the excavation of Combe-Capelle. It was necessary, however, to make some small alterations. First, not all of the analytical data are reproduced in the software, primarily because of the more esoteric nature of some of the observations we made. A complete data set in computerized format can be obtained from Dibble and McPherron (1996).

The second alteration was made to provide students with more flexibility in designing their own projects. During the actual excavation we opened up a series of units and excavated most of these to bedrock. However, our excavation was fairly limited in extent, and we did not think it would be particularly interesting for students to excavate exactly where we did. This creates a problem in that we don't know what is to be found in the parts of the site where we did not excavate.

Our solution to this problem was to create a simulated site based on the samples we excavated from our units. The *Virtual Dig* site areas corresponding to our site sectors match, in probabilistic terms, what we found in those sectors in terms of the stratigraphic levels, the depth of deposits, the density of artifacts, their orientations, and the overall composition of the assemblages. Thus, what a student excavates from a particular unit will not be identical to what we found, but it will be very close to our findings in that general area. If the actual Combe-Capelle data are used and analyzed, the results will match the published results (Dibble and Lenoir 1995).

A NOTE TO INSTRUCTORS:
USING *VIRTUAL DIG* IN INTRODUCTORY CLASSES

Our goal in developing *Virtual Dig* was to provide students with a realistic experience of what it is like to excavate a prehistoric site. Of course, digging is what most people think of when they think about archaeology. But we all know that digging is but one aspect of the overall process. Before you dig you have to develop some understanding of the time period(s) represented in the site, you have to know how to analyze the material that you will recover, and you have to develop a realistic strategy for the fieldwork (including deciding on personnel, equipment, and logistics). In its attempt to achieve realism, *Virtual Dig* includes all of those other aspects, in addition to providing an accurate feel for artifact recovery.

This would seem to raise a problem in using *Virtual Dig* in an introductory class, however. The simple fact is that students at this level of experience do not yet have the necessary background or even the interest to successfully plan for an excavation and deal quantitatively with the results. And most instructors would not wish to spend an entire semester working through these issues and thereby ignoring the usual coverage of culture sequences and other topics that are often covered in such classes.

Fortunately, *Virtual Dig* can be used in different ways. Keep in mind that the program is organized as a series of modules that cover the various phases of preparation, excavation, and analysis. If students follow these modules in their correct order, they will be led through the entire research project (what we call the virtual project). This is one way of using *Virtual Dig*—perhaps the most obvious way—but it may or may not be the most useful approach for all classes. Then again, each module is completely independent of the others, and it is possible to use any single one or combination of them in the context of a course in order to focus on the aspects that are most relevant. The choice of modules will vary among instructors, and experience will help to determine which ones work best in different contexts.

Background

The Background module is beneficial to anyone using the program, especially in helping students to come up with a research design that would be appropriate for this site.

Site Setup

The Setup module is both informative and fun for students at every level because it addresses questions regarding everything from tools to use, vehicles to buy or lease, food and lodging, personnel, and the like.

Because of the way the program is presented, it is easy to get the impression that an approved budget is necessary before excavation can begin. This is not true, however, and students can use the Excavation module at any time.

Excavation

Interactive excavation is, to a point, ideal for giving students in introductory classes a realistic feel for doing archaeology. If you are going to have your students do any serious digging, however, be sure that they understand how to use the automatic excavation feature of the program and that in using automatic excavation on a square you can tell the program to follow the same stratigraphy as in an adjacent square. That way, once you figure out the stratigraphy by hand-excavating one square, the program can take over from there to do other squares. Automatic excavation can also dig in arbitrary levels.

The Excavation module can be used in several different ways in an introductory class:

1. Have students excavate a trench to find the limits of the site in one direction. They should start from the existing trench and work their way out.
2. Ask students to excavate adjacent squares with two or three different tools, monitoring how much time it takes to excavate a whole square by hand with a trowel versus a shovel, for example, but then also noting the difference in artifact recovery.
3. Divide your class into teams, with each team assigned to deal with different parts of the site (the biggest differences are apparent as one goes up the hill rather than across). This is a bigger project, however, and will require that the students get into analysis of the material.

Lithics Lab

Our experience with the Lithics Lab module in introductory classes has been quite good. Students enjoy two parts of this section the most: Learning the Types and the Flintknapper Primer, which is a flintknapping simulator.

Although a little esoteric, lithics make a good material with which to illustrate basic typological concepts. We kept the approach to lithic typology relatively straightforward and organized it in such a way that students can readily see what kinds of characteristics define different types. Like many archaeological typologies, Bordes's lithics types are somewhat arbitrary, which helps to stimulate discussions concerning the underlying reality of archaeological types and the limits of using them to make inferences about the past. If your introductory class deals with any stone tool cultures, this module gets as close as you can to hands-on experience.

For understanding what's involved in stone tool technology, the flintknapping simulator allows students—in a bloodless way!—to make their own flakes and then retouch them into recognizable types. The variables that they control in flaked production are the ones identified in controlled experiments as among the most important, which means that this module can be useful even in advanced lithics classes. But for students of any level, the retouching section is just plain fun. You might try to have a competition among the students to see who can produce the "best" stone tool, with the entire class voting on the submissions. This is a fun way to introduce students to a technology they have heard about but with which they have no firsthand experience.

Analysis

The Analysis module is probably the most difficult to incorporate into an introductory class, simply because the quantitative background of most students at this level is so limited. Although the program makes it easy to produce tables and charts to compare different levels or areas of the site, the need to deal with admittedly abstract lithic observations can be daunting.

One thing that is easy for students in an introductory class to do is to determine what type of Mousterian is present at the site, defined according to the overall proportions of different lithic types. Students can compare their assemblages graphically to idealized Mousterian assemblage types in order to determine the kind of Mousterian they have.

Note: Bear in mind that students need not analyze their own excavated assemblages. Instead, they can base their analyses on the original Combe-Capelle data set. That way, given the above comments about the drudgery of excavation, they can explore basic analysis without spending too much time collecting the data.

Background to the Middle Paleolithic

2

Virtual Dig is based on the French Middle Paleolithic site of Combe-Capelle and uses data generated during recent excavations there. However, before we describe Combe-Capelle (see Chapter 3), it is useful first to summarize our understanding of the European Middle Paleolithic. As you read the text in this chapter and the next, you can look at slides of some of the topics on the CD-ROM. From the main menu, choose the **Background/The Middle Paleolithic** option and click on the slide names on the left-hand side of the screen to see different pictures.

THE MIDDLE PALEOLITHIC

The Middle Paleolithic dates from about 250,000 to 35,000 years ago and coincides with the latter part of the Pleistocene epoch, or Ice Age. The term *Paleolithic* means Old Stone Age, and, as the name implies, the principal kinds of artifacts recovered from Paleolithic sites are lithics (stone tools and the byproducts of their manufacture). The Middle Paleolithic has traditionally been defined as a flake tool industry, which was meant to differentiate it from earlier Acheulian industries (characterized by the presence of bifaces, or handaxes) and later Upper Paleolithic industries (characterized by blades and blade tools).

Our understanding of this time period is based on the excavation of a large number of caves and some open-air sites throughout the Old World, including Europe, Asia, Africa, and the Near East. In addition to the analysis of stone tools and bones recovered at these sites, geological studies and the analysis of prehistoric pollen play a key role in interpreting the Middle Paleolithic, as they provide information on what the climate was like when the sites were occupied.

DATING AND ENVIRONMENT

The Pleistocene, which lasted for about 2 million years, was characterized by cyclical variation in climate over periods of approximately 100,000 years. During the colder, or glacial, periods massive buildups of ice occurred,

The Paleolithic site
of La Ferrassie

primarily in the northern latitudes and higher elevations. During the warmer periods, or interglacials, the ice retreated and conditions became more temperate as in modern, or Holocene, times (which began around 10,000 years ago). Traditional frameworks for Pleistocene chronology were based on terrestrial evidence of glacial advance (and associated changes in flora, fauna, and sediments), whereas current chronology is based on fluctuations in two isotopes of oxygen (O^{18} and O^{16}) found in shells taken from deep-sea cores. On this basis a numbered series of oxygen-isotope stages have been defined, with even-numbered stages representing cold periods and odd-numbered ones representing warm periods (see figure on page 11). At this point it appears that the underlying mechanism for these regular cycles of global climatic change relates to variation in solar energy that the earth receives. These variations in solar energy are brought about by cyclical variations in the earth's orbit.

During maximum glacial times, ice sheets, sometimes several miles thick, covered relatively large areas of the Northern Hemisphere. This was associated with a rather dramatic drop in temperature: In northern Europe, for example, average mid-summer temperatures may have been as low as 5° C (41° F), and the temperature may have been below freezing for much of the year. These effects varied depending on latitude and elevation. Likewise, in direct response to the buildup of the ice sheets, global sea levels dropped considerably, as much as 130 m (425 ft) below the present level, which exposed large areas of previously submerged coastline.

As the climate changed during the various cold and warm cycles of the Pleistocene, many aspects of the environment changed, including the nature of the vegetation and faunal communities. When temperatures dropped, the forests of western and central Europe were replaced by more open vegetation communities, characterized as either tundra or steppe, although some localized stands of pine, birch, or willow remained. Coupled with this was a change in the faunal communities, as more open-habitat species moved in, including reindeer (caribou) and specialized cold-loving fauna such as the woolly mammoth, woolly rhi-

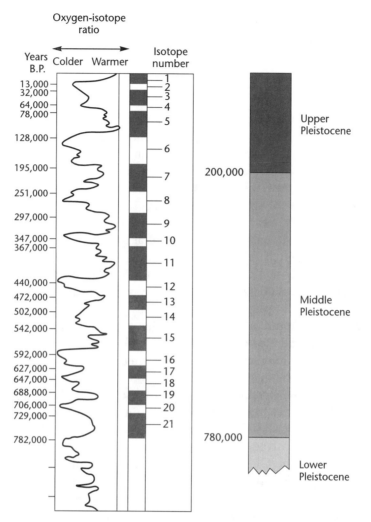

Oxygen-isotope
ratio

Years
B.P.   Colder   Warmer

Isotope
number

Pleistocene glacial
chronology based on
oxygen-isotope ratios
in marine sediments.
Notice the many oscil-
lations between cold
and warm phases.
(Data from Shackleton and
Opdyke, 1973)

Odd-numbered stages (shaded areas) = warmer periods, less glacial ice cover
Even-numbered stages = colder periods, more glacial ice cover

noceros, arctic hare, and arctic fox. With a return to more temperate conditions there was a succession of tree colonizations, from birch, pine, and spruce to full deciduous forests of oak, hazel, and elm that are common today. Typical interglacial faunas were also similar to those occurring in various regions today. For example, in Europe these faunas include red deer (elk), deer, moose, bison, wild cattle, and pigs. In fact, some of the interglacial periods had climatic conditions that were even milder than today. During the last, or Eem, interglacial (oxygen-isotope Stage 5e), sea level rose to around 6–10 m (20–32 ft) higher than at present, and semitropical species such as hippopotamus inhabited northern Europe. We use the term *paleoenvironment* to refer to the past environment reconstructed using geological, pollen, and faunal studies.

Dating Middle Paleolithic sites is difficult. Radiocarbon dating extends reliably to 30,000 years ago, but use of the tandem mass accelerator can push it as far back as 50,000 years ago. New techniques, such as thermoluminescence dating of burned flint and electron spin resonance dating of teeth, have the potential to date objects much older, but these techniques are still in the experimental stages. Much of the dating of Middle Paleolithic sites is thus based on geological and other paleoenvironmental evidence, which can help indicate the stage of the Pleistocene that is represented.

NEANDERTALS

Neandertals are a group of hominids that were present throughout much of the Old World during the Middle Paleolithic. The Neandertals have very distinct physical features, including large brains, sloping foreheads, large brow ridges, large faces and noses, large front teeth (often with evidence of heavy wear indicating that the teeth were used as tools), and robust bones (suggesting that Neandertals were heavily muscled). Most specialists believe that Neandertals originated about 250,000 years ago from an ancestral hominid form known as *Homo erectus*.

For many years it was thought that the Middle Paleolithic was synonymous with Neandertals. More recently, however, it has been shown that this is not universally true. In Europe, virtually all of the hominids found in association with Middle Paleolithic stone tool industries are Neandertals. In southwestern Asia and Africa, however, both Neandertals and anatomically modern *Homo sapiens* have been found in Middle Paleolithic contexts, demonstrating that the present-day independence between human biological variability and behavior (as expressed in culture and technology) existed as far back as the Middle Paleolithic.

One of the biggest debates concerning this time period is the place of Neandertals within hominid evolution. Two schools of thought exist concerning this debate. The first, the multiregional continuity hypothesis, argues that Neandertals and other archaic *Homo sapiens* and their associated Middle Paleolithic tool assemblages evolved into modern *Homo sapiens* and Upper Paleolithic industries throughout the Old World at more or less the same time. Similarities in skeletal characteristics between archaic (including Neandertal) and modern fossil remains have been used to support this hypothesis. The second, the replacement hypothesis, argues that one population of modern humans, most likely residing in Africa, evolved and spread throughout the Old World, eventually replacing aboriginal Neandertal populations. Fossil remains from Africa and mitochondrial and nuclear DNA studies have been used to support this hypothesis.

A related question is whether Neandertals represent a different species, *Homo neanderthalensis*. This debate began with the first discovery of Neandertals in the middle of the nineteenth century and revolves around the significance of the morphological differences in the skeletons of Neandertals and moderns and the behavioral differences as interpreted on the basis of archaeological remains from Neandertal sites. These topics continue to cause considerable debate and are the focus of a great deal of ongoing research.

MOUSTERIAN STONE TOOLS

Several different Middle Paleolithic industries existed throughout the Old World, but in western Europe the Middle Paleolithic is represented by the Mousterian, named after the French site of Le Moustier, located not far from Combe-Capelle.

Typologically, that is, in terms of the types of stone tools represented, Middle Paleolithic assemblages are often composed of two major classes: scrapers, and notches and denticulates. Scrapers are tools that exhibit continuous and generally smooth retouching along one or more (usually lateral) edges. As we will learn later, many different types of scrapers are recognized in the typology of the

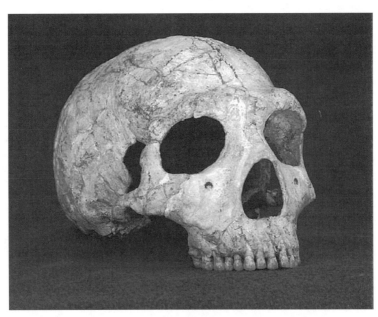

Lower and Middle Paleolithic developed by the French archaeologist François Bordes. Bordes identified 63 different tool types based on tool shape, the technique of manufacture, and edge modification. The scraper types are differentiated on the basis of how many and which edges are retouched and on the basis of the shape of the retouched edges.

Notches and denticulates make up the second most prevalent tool type. Notches are flakes that have a relatively deep concavity along an edge produced either by a single blow or a series of fine retouch removals. Denticulates are tools that have two or more adjacent notches along an edge.

The third, though much less common, tool type is bifaces. Bifaces (also called handaxes) are tools that are retouched on both surfaces. Although much rarer than scrapers or notches and denticulates, they are significant in terms of Middle Paleolithic industrial systematics.

A distinct flaking technology associated with many Middle Paleolithic industries is Levallois, a prepared core technique. Although the exact definition of Levallois has become the subject of intense debate, the idea behind the original concept is that the surface of a core is prepared in a special way in order to remove a flake with a desired shape. There are many varieties of Levallois that are differentiated on the basis of the steps involved in preparing the core surface and the kinds of shapes achieved (for example, flakes, blades or elongated flakes, or points).

Using his typology, Bordes divided Mousterian assemblages from French Paleolithic sites into different kinds of Mousterian based on his observation that certain tool types were consistently found together within deposits:

- *Charentian Mousterian* is characterized by a high percentage of scrapers. Bordes identified two subvariants of the Charentian based on the presence or absence of Levallois flakes: (1) The Quina Mousterian, named after the site of La Quina, exhibits a low percentage of Levallois; and (2) the Ferrassie Mousterian, named after the site of La Ferrassie, has a higher percentage of Levallois. Some other differences exist between the Quina and Ferrassie Mousterian in terms of the types of scrapers typically associated with each.

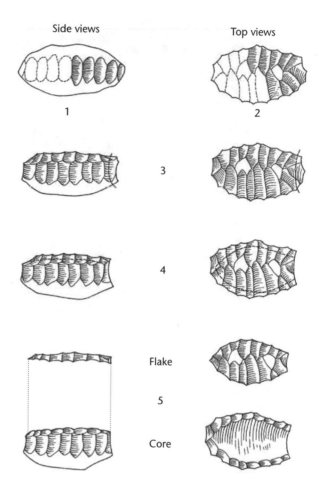

Steps involved in the manufacture of a Levallois flake (After Bordaz 1970)

Side views   Top views

1   2

3

4

Flake

5

Core

- *Denticulate Mousterian* is characterized by a high percentage of notched tools (notches and denticulates) and a low percentage of scrapers, but with varying amounts of Levallois flakes.

- *Typical Mousterian* is characterized by a moderate amount of notched tools and scrapers and varying amounts of Levallois flakes.

- *Mousterian of Acheulian Tradition (MTA)* is distinguished from the other groups by having bifaces, in which it resembles an earlier industry, the Acheulian, which was prevalent throughout the middle part of the Pleistocene. Two sub-variants of the MTA exist. MTA Type A assemblages are much like Typical Mousterian assemblages but with the addition of bifaces, whereas MTA Type B assemblages are more like Denticulate Mousterian but with bifaces. Either kind of MTA assemblage can contain varying amounts of Levallois technique.

Beginning in the 1960s, the meaning of this variation in Mousterian assemblages developed into one of the most hotly contested issues in Paleolithic research. Bordes viewed these variants as representing distinct, though contemporary, cultural groups that interacted throughout the long duration of the Middle Paleolithic (Bordes 1961a, 1973). In 1966, American archaeologists Lewis Binford and Sally Binford suggested that these variants reflected different activities that were being performed (for example, Denticulate Mousterian was thought to be associated

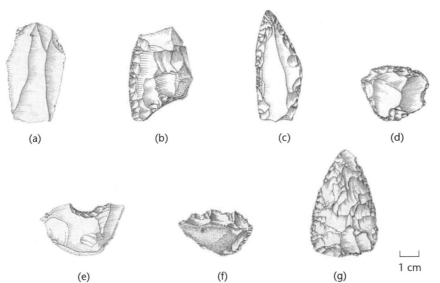

(a)   (b)   (c)   (d)

(e)   (f)   (g)

1 cm

Common Middle Paleolithic tools: (a) Levallois flake, (b) convex single scraper, (c) convex convergent scraper, (d) convex transverse scraper, (e) notch, (f) denticulate, (g) biface

with bone- and woodworking). This led to what is generally referred to as the "Bordes-Binford Debate," which became famous within archaeology circles because it represented a classic dilemma in archaeological interpretation: Are differences in contemporary archaeological assemblages due to style or function?

At about the same time, the English archaeologist Paul Mellars (1965, 1969) proposed that some of the different Mousterian assemblages were temporally distinct, that is, they occurred at different times. Citing the stratigraphic patterning seen at several sites, he noted that MTA is most often on top of a sequence, and that within the Charentian, Quina Mousterian assemblages are almost always located above (that is, later in time than) Ferrassie ones.

Recent work, in part based on ethnographic accounts of existing peoples who still use stone tools, has suggested that these assemblage differences relate to something completely different. Nicolas Rolland and Harold Dibble (1990) have proposed that many of the tool types identified by Bordes are the result of differences in tool reduction due to resharpening rather than predefined tool types. For example, one type of scraper can be turned into another type just by resharpening it. Likewise, a notch can be converted into a denticulate by adding a second notch next to the first. These differences in the degree of reduction can be the result of a range of factors including how far and how often groups were moving, how long they were staying at a site, and how much raw material was available in the area around the site. Rolland and Dibble suggest that the more intensely utilized industries are often represented by the Quina and Ferrassie Mousterian groups, whereas the least intensely utilized are, for example, the Denticulate Mousterian. Thus these groups are not discrete entities but rather are somewhat arbitrary points along a continuum reflecting intensity of utilization, as reflected in the degree of core reduction, tool production, and tool reduction.

LIFE IN THE MIDDLE PALEOLITHIC

The Middle Paleolithic is characterized by sites that represent an accumulation of artifacts that were, in many cases, deposited over long periods of time. Traditionally there has been a heavy bias on the part of Middle Paleolithic researchers in favor of excavating cave sites, largely because they were believed to have better preserved and longer sequences of cultural deposits. It is now clear, however, that Middle Paleolithic sites occur in a variety of settings. Cave and rockshelter deposits are numerous, but many open-air sites have been found and may be more typical of the period. In general, most western European Middle Paleolithic sites appear to be habitation sites represented by a wide range of tool types and faunal remains; however, some sites may represent more specialized economic activities. Among these more specialized sites are those where animals were killed and butchered for food or those related to obtaining raw material or manufacturing stone tools. Middle Paleolithic sites are generally small, usually less than 1,000 sq m. In cave or rockshelter sites, the size may be related directly to the constraints of the shelter, but even open-air sites are generally small. Based on ethnographic analogy and site size, researchers believe that Middle Paleolithic peoples were organized in small bands of perhaps 15–20 individuals.

Although there is a tendency among some archaeologists to interpret their sites as so-called living floors, most sites have suffered a significant degree of post-depositional disturbance; in fact, some "sites" have been shown to be the result of redeposition by stream action rather than human occupation. This is why taphonomy, the study of site formation and its effects on the artifacts and other remains found in sites, is becoming a major part of Paleolithic research.

Because of the age of the deposits, most Middle Paleolithic sites preserve little in the way of subsistence information other than animal bones. It is almost certain that wild plant products composed a significant portion of the hominid diet, but determining the exact proportion is largely guesswork. Some progress has been made on the basis of analyses of trace elements in hominid bones, however. Although cooking utensils have not been found, the fact that hearths are known from this period suggests that some cooking of meat was done.

One of the major debates since the mid-1970s concerns the extent to which Middle Paleolithic hominids relied on hunting versus scavenging to obtain meat (there is no evidence of domesticated animals). Animal remains are often abundant in Middle Paleolithic sites, and traditionally it has been assumed that they represent prey acquired through purposeful hunting. This assumption has been called into question, not only for the Middle Paleolithic but also for the Lower Paleolithic. However, most specialists now agree that hunting played a major, if not exclusive, role in Middle Paleolithic meat acquisition. The principal game exploited during the Middle Paleolithic differed in relation to both climate and the local environment. Archaeological evidence indicates that Middle Paleolithic peoples depended on a range of small- to large-sized herbivores, including bison, horses, and reindeer. No evidence has been found indicating that they regularly exploited fish, shellfish, and birds.

Probably no aspect of Middle Paleolithic behavior has received more attention in the recent literature than the extent to which groups used symbolic expression and whether that expression took the form of language, religion, symbolic rituals, or art. The general lack of evidence of symbolic expression could be due either to poor preservation or to our lack of recognition of symbolic expression. Most evidence argued to represent symbolic behavior is later shown to be the result of natural agencies or simply an overly romantic interpretation. This then raises the question of whether Middle Paleolithic "culture" was fully modern, and on this subject a great deal of debate exists. Likewise, the question of whether Middle Paleolithic peoples had language has been addressed from a number of lines of evidence, including primate ethology, animal psychology, and analyses of fossil hominid bones and stone tools. The question remains open.

To date, there is no unambiguous evidence that Middle Paleolithic peoples had specific religious beliefs or practiced any kind of religious or ritualistic ceremonies. Virtually all of the artifacts found in Middle Paleolithic contexts are utilitarian in nature, and the lack of any kind of representational art prevents us from reconstructing specific belief systems. Although there has been much speculation about a "Cave Bear Cult" during the Middle Paleolithic, research has shown that the evidence used to support this notion is the result of natural agencies. Some evidence, primarily from Europe, indicates that cannibalism was practiced. The evidence consists of human bones that exhibit either what have been interpreted as cutmarks or signs of burning.

The question of Middle Paleolithic burials has been debated since the middle of the twentieth century, and consensus is still lacking as to whether burial was practiced. In Europe relatively few sites have provided clear evidence of purposeful burial, and this evidence has been questioned primarily on the basis of the lack of rigor in presentation. In contrast, the relatively high degree of preservation of some hominid skeletons has been used as an argument for deliberate burial. In the Near East a relatively larger number of convincing burials exists. Even if it is accepted that there are Middle Paleolithic burials, the question remains as to whether they reflect a religious belief or ceremony. Primarily at issue has been the lack of associated items that could be interpreted as grave goods; Middle Paleolithic burials typically contain the same mundane items found throughout the site.

The question of Middle Paleolithic personal ornamentation has also been debated for many years. Several examples of "curiosities" have been found in Middle Paleolithic sites, including fossil shells, marine shells, and minerals. Several examples of ochre (iron oxide and manganese) have been found in Middle Paleolithic contexts from both Europe and the Near East. In later periods ochre is often used in coloring and art, and it may have been used for that purpose in the Middle Paleolithic, although no direct evidence of such use is known. Some animal bones exhibit holes that have been interpreted as intentional piercing, either to serve as an attachment for cord or to produce musical sounds. Most of these examples have been shown to be the result of natural agents such as chewing by carnivores.

The Middle Paleolithic is thus a fascinating time period from a number of points of view. Clearly it represents an important stage in the history of human technology. As a period that took place just before the development of unquestioned modern anatomy and behavior, it serves as an important point of reference for understanding our evolutionary roots.

Suggested Readings

Binford 1973; Binford and Binford 1966; Bordes 1972; Chase and Dibble 1987; Dibble and Mellars 1992; Gargett 1989; Laville, Rigaud, and Sackett 1980; Mellars 1996; Stringer and Gamble 1993; Trinkaus and Shipman 1993

Combe-Capelle

3

Combe-Capelle is located in the Couze River valley. Couze River is a small tributary of the Dordogne, in southwestern France. Combe-Capelle consists of at least four distinct sites located on a limestone cliff. On the plateau surface at the top of the cliff (called the Plateau de Ruffet), a large open-air site contains Lower, Middle, and Upper Paleolithic remains. At the base of the cliff just at the edge of the plateau are two sites. The Abri Peyrony is a rockshelter that contains primarily Middle Paleolithic material. The other site, the Roc de Combe-Capelle, contains primarily Upper Paleolithic remains, although some Mousterian is also present. This site is best known for the recovery of a modern *Homo sapiens* skeleton in the Upper Paleolithic deposits. The fourth site, Combe-Capelle Bas, is located at the base of the cliff and contains primarily Middle Paleolithic remains. Because we are concerned only with the fourth site in *Virtual Dig,* we will refer to it simply as Combe-Capelle.

Although Combe-Capelle was discovered in the late 1800s, the first major excavations were carried out in the 1920s by a French Canadian named Henri-Marc Ami. Ami's excavations began in 1926 and over four years he dug a 35-m-long (115 ft) trench going uphill from the base of the slope. He defined a series of stratigraphic layers (Levels I–V) and collected tools from each level. Unfortunately, Ami died in 1931 before he was able to publish the results of his work. Twenty years later, Maurice Bourgon undertook the task of publishing Ami's results, but he also died before his manuscript was published (Bourgon 1957). Nonetheless, what we knew about the Combe-Capelle Bas sequence came primarily from Bourgon's work. Based primarily on the collection of tools saved by Ami, Bourgon suggested that the lower levels of Combe-Capelle (especially Level IV) represented a Quina Mousterian. He classified Level III as a Ferrassie Mousterian and Level I as an MTA industry rich in Levallois flakes.

The site was reexcavated beginning in 1987 under the direction of Harold Dibble (one of the authors of this text) and his French colleague, Michel Lenoir of the Université de Bordeaux. We conducted these excavations to answer several research questions. Because the original excavations occurred before modern methods of dating and geology were developed,

General view of Combe-Capelle during excavation

little was known about the geological and chronological context of the excavated assemblages. The industrial sequence of assemblages at Combe-Capelle did not match those observed at other Middle Paleolithic sites in the area, especially that the Quina Mousterian was beneath, and therefore earlier than, the Ferrassie. We therefore designed excavations to obtain a good stratigraphic sample of artifacts to determine the reasons for this apparent anomaly. In addition, Combe-Capelle sits on a source of high-quality flint, enabling us to examine the influence of raw material availability on the artifact assemblage composition. These research questions dictated our excavation strategy and the types of analysis we performed.

We obtained funding for these excavations from several sources. The National Science Foundation funded the major portion of the work, and we also obtained funding from the University of Pennsylvania and private donors.

Excavations began in 1987 following an initial season of mapping and surveying and continued to 1990, followed by a study season in 1991 to complete the lithic analysis. We excavated three sectors at Combe-Capelle to sample the full extent of Ami's trench and to obtain a representative sample of the geological beds that he excavated and the tool assemblage from each bed.

During the initial excavations in 1987, we located the edges of Ami's trench, which had been obliterated by vegetation and slumping of the backdirt left from his earlier excavation. Fortunately the contact with intact deposits was relatively easy to define because the backdirt was much looser than the intact soil. We dry screened the backdirt through 1/4-in mesh screen as it was excavated to get a sample of material that Ami threw out, as it was a common practice in the early 1900s to keep only complete tools or good examples of tools.

Once we identified the edges of Ami's trench, we set up several excavation units next to it. We excavated two units in Sector I at the base of the limestone cliff and Ami's trench. We excavated one deep unit, A1, to provide a sample of artifacts and profile of the geological beds in the lower portion of the site and to locate bedrock. We excavated an adjacent unit, A2, along the west side of Ami's trench. In Sector II, a series of 1 × 1-m units were excavated perpendicular to Ami's trench, running west from his trench edge. The goal of our excavations in

Stratigraphy of Combe-Capelle as defined by Ami

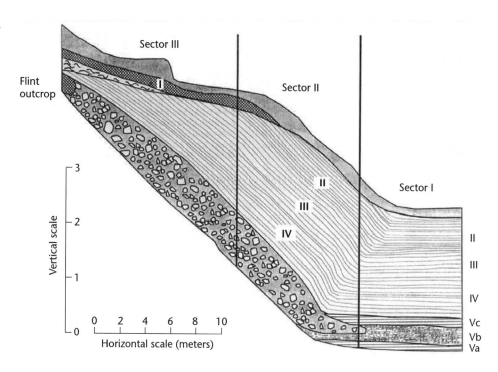

this sector was to expose front and side profiles of the deposits to get a sample of industries and geological beds in the middle part of the trench. We excavated Sector III in the upper part of Ami's trench adjacent to the east edge of the trench in an area where the Level I MTA deposits were found. There we excavated two units, C1 and D1.

We used trowels to excavate deposits and placed dirt in a bucket for screening. We mapped in and assigned a unique identification (ID) number to all artifacts and bones over 3 cm (1.2 in) in size. We also mapped the center of the area where the fill of each bucket was excavated, giving provenience information to the small flakes and bones recovered in it. We mapped all natural rocks larger than a fist to aid in interpreting site geology.

We used a laser theodolite and electronic distance meter for the mapping, which made it quick and accurate. The theodolite was linked to a portable laptop computer, and all provenience information was transferred directly to the laptop. At the end of the day, we transferred the data to the main computer at the lab, where data could be checked for accuracy and a map of the site was continually updated.

Descriptions of the geological deposits were made by the archaeologists working with the sediments and by the project geologists. Level changes were marked by changes in color, texture, and cobble content. The levels were given preliminary level designations in the field; these could be refined as they were completed and a profile was drawn, and any changes could be input directly into the computer database. A geologist also visited the site during the excavations to draw profile maps of the completed sectors and to describe the deposits in geological terms.

After we excavated the buckets and artifacts, they were taken to the field laboratory, located in a building approximately 2 km (1.2 mi) from the site. There the artifacts were washed and labeled. The bucket fill was screened through 1-cm

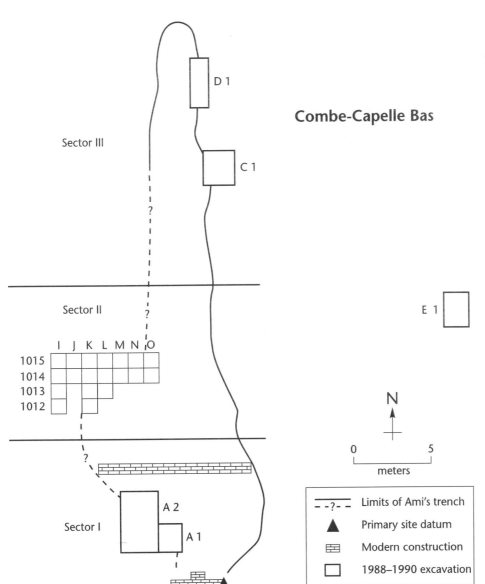

Map of Combe-Capelle showing outline of Ami's trench and the location of the excavation units

Combe-Capelle Bas

(.4-in) mesh screen, and half of the buckets were also screened through 2.5-mm (.1-in) mesh. Two provenience tags for each bucket were printed in the field; one tag was marked "coarse" and was placed in a small plastic bag in a drying tray in which material from the 1-cm mesh screen was placed. The second tag was marked "fine," and the same process was followed for material from the 2.5-mm mesh. This material was then dried and sorted.

Lithic analysis was conducted in the laboratory, and all data were entered into laptop computers and later transferred to the main database where statistical analysis was performed. The analysis focused on technological and typological aspects of the assemblage. Variables such as flake type, platform type, cortex, tool type, and metric measurements were recorded for each stone artifact. Small flakes recovered from the screens were not analyzed individually, but material from each bucket was weighed and counted to get information on the density of small finds in each level. Because bone preservation was extremely poor, detailed faunal analysis was not done.

The final analysis of the data was completed when we returned to the United States. The results of our work revealed that Ami's original assessment of the stratified deposits at Combe-Capelle was biased by his policy of collecting complete and "good" tools and discarding others. With a better understanding of the industries, we found that the sequence at Combe-Capelle was not reversed, and in fact, there was no true Quina, Ferrassie, or even MTA at the site. We will not tell you now what kind of Mousterian assemblage was present, because you will soon be able to determine that for yourself.

The abundance of raw material at Combe-Capelle resulted in the production of large blanks that could be transported. Paleolithic groups did not visit the site specifically to gather raw material, as many other tools were found indicating that other activities were taking place at the site. The use of the high-quality flint at Combe-Capelle appears to have been rather opportunistic—something that groups took advantage of during their movements through the area, most likely in pursuit of game.

Suggested Readings

Dibble and Lenoir 1995; Dibble and McPherron 1996

Research Design 4

This chapter and the next six provide you with information on how to set up an excavation project. This workbook and the CD-ROM will take you through a series of topics and exercises designed to teach you the basics of planning a field project. You will learn how to write a research design, place excavation units, decide what methods of artifact recovery and proveniencing you will use, choose your project personnel, deal with logistical concerns, and develop a project budget. These are steps you will take in planning any field project, but we have used examples from our work at Combe-Capelle to illustrate how a field project is put together. The importance of setting up your field project cannot be overemphasized, as it sets the stage for how you will excavate and what data you will recover during excavation.

Eventually you will design your own virtual project, excavate the site, and analyze the data you recover to answer research questions you develop during the setup phase. The ultimate goal of these chapters is to prepare a proposal to excavate Combe-Capelle in order to answer your research questions and to come up with a budget that will be approved by our virtual funding agency.

WHAT IS A RESEARCH DESIGN?

A research design is essentially a guide to fieldwork. It is the plan that you follow as you set about doing a field project, and it guides the fieldwork, the analysis, and the write-up. The basis of your research design is a set of research questions to be addressed during fieldwork and analysis; these questions help you determine where to dig, how to dig, and what types of analyses to perform. The research design can also be used as a planning document for determining the length of the field season, the size of the crew, and, hence, the budget.

Keep in mind that each archaeological site is unique and is destroyed during the process of excavation. Therefore, in addition to addressing specific research questions, you need to document as much information as possible and to be thorough in your collection of material so that it is available for future research. It is also important to remain flexible when developing your research design, especially if you are going to be working in an area that is unknown to you. The research design can and should be modified continually as fieldwork progresses and more information is obtained.

FORMULATING A RESEARCH DESIGN

You should take two important steps in order to develop a successful research design: conduct background research and obtain necessary permits and permission to excavate.

Background Research

The first step is to conduct background research on the site, the area in which you will be working, and the theoretical problem you will address. The background research should include a relatively detailed literature search on what has been done previously at your site and in areas that are similar to the one you are working in. You should also research the general topic you will be addressing with your research (in this case, the Middle Paleolithic). This information can come from archives, published archaeological reports, contract archaeology reports, historic documents, or museum collections.

Information on the site environment should be obtained as part of your background research, including information on the present-day environment (for planning the logistics of the fieldwork) and the paleoenvironment. You should obtain information on floral and faunal resources, topography, geology, and water. Floral and faunal resources can provide you with information on the availability and diversity of food sources; the topography may have dictated where a site was located or may have provided certain constraints on site size; the geology can tell you about the potential for buried deposits, the preservation within those deposits, whether the remains you will encounter are intact or disturbed, and the availability of lithic source material. Water was a critical resource to prehistoric and historic groups, and most archaeological sites with evidence of habitation or camping are found near water sources. The location and nature of water sources will be important in helping you determine what a site was used for.

Permits or Permission to Excavate a Site

The second step you should take before writing your research design is to obtain permission to excavate the site. If the site is on private land, you should obtain written permission from the landowner. If it is on public land, you should apply for a permit from the applicable public agency (for example, the U.S. Bureau of Land Management or the U.S. Forest Service). In most cases, government agencies require a research design as part of the permit application; you should inquire about their requirements before you write your design or plan your project. If you are working in the United States, you should also consult with any Native American groups that are in the area or claim ancestry to the site, so that they can be involved in the formulation of the research design and fieldwork strategy from the beginning. According to the 1990 Native American Graves Protection and Repatriation Act, before you excavate on federal land you must consult with Native American groups claiming cultural affiliation to prehistoric remains concerning what should be done if human remains are encountered during excavation. Many states have similar laws covering state land.

WRITING A RESEARCH DESIGN

The research design should be written in a concise, easy-to-understand format. The following items should be included in your written research design:

- Summary of background research describing the site, previous archaeological work at the site or in the vicinity of the site, and the environment or paleoenvironment.
- Detailed research questions (hypotheses) that can be answered during fieldwork. It is also useful to specify the types of information you will need in order to answer these questions, and you may want to explain why the particular site you are excavating is a good candidate for answering the research questions you have developed.
- Description of your field and lab methods. How will you get the data? How will they be analyzed? You should include information on your excavation strategy (excavation units, proveniencing, screening), what you can learn from the kinds of analyses you plan to do, and what kind of samples you will be taking to send to specialists (for example, pollen or dating samples). You should include a discussion of your plans for dealing with human remains in this section, if applicable.
- Schedule for completion of the fieldwork, analysis, and final report. This is often referred to as a scope or plan of work.
- Budget for conducting the field project.

RESEARCH DESIGN AT COMBE-CAPELLE

At Combe-Capelle we relied on archival documents from Ami's excavations at the site and examined artifact collections from these projects that were housed in museums in France. We also read literature published on Paleolithic sites in the Perigord region, on the Paleolithic of France, and on the Middle and Upper Paleolithic in general to help us develop our research questions and plan our field project. We examined the available paleoenvironmental data for the region around the site and consulted with specialists familiar with the geology and climatic history of the area. Authorization for our excavation came from several sources. Because the site was on private land, we had to get authorization from the property owner. We also had to get permission from the regional director of antiquities and the French Ministry of Culture.

We addressed two basic research questions during our work at Combe-Capelle. The first question concerned the typological sequence of industries at Combe-Capelle. When Ami excavated the site, he found an industrial sequence of assemblages that did not match those observed at other Middle Paleolithic sites in the area, a fact that made Combe-Capelle unique (see Chapter 3). We wanted to obtain a sufficient sample of stone tools from the stratigraphic levels at Combe-Capelle to determine the sequence of lithic industries.

The second question concerned how raw materials were used at Combe-Capelle. The site is located on a source of high-quality flint, which enabled us to examine the influence of raw material availability on lithic technology and typology. We were specifically interested in determining if Combe-Capelle had been used as a quarry site.

Suggested Readings

Binford 1964; Struever 1971

EXERCISE 4.1

Defining Research Questions for Your Virtual Project

To start your virtual project, you will need to come up with research questions that you will attempt to answer by excavating Combe-Capelle. For each question, discuss briefly why you would want to know the answer and what kinds of data you would need to answer the question.

After you have shown these questions to your instructor and they have been approved, you will use them to guide your excavation and analysis.

Unit Definition and Placement

5

A variety of units can be used on an excavation project, and the types of units you choose and their location on the site will significantly affect the amount and quality of the data you recover. Each type of unit will provide a different degree of exposure; each has advantages and disadvantages. The types of units you choose and where you put them will be based on your research questions, time and budget constraints, and the nature of the site (for example, topography, vegetation, site type). As with many of the other decisions you will make when excavating, you should decide on the type of excavation unit(s) you will use before you go into the field in order to help you plan your time and crew size. It is important, however, that you remain flexible. As you recover material, you may find that different unit types will be more useful for the particular site you are digging.

Archaeologists use units during excavation to maintain control of the material they excavate and to secure good provenience information. Units are especially important if you are not point proveniencing (that is, measuring in the exact location of each object), because they provide the context of the artifacts and features that is crucial for archaeological interpretation. Units also preserve stratigraphic sections that can be used to guide further excavation.

SITE GRID

The first thing you will have to set up on an archaeological site is the site grid, which is like a Cartesian coordinate system for the site as a whole, with X (horizontal) and Y (vertical) axes. Grids are established from the primary site datum (PSD), a permanent point on the site from which all measurements are taken. Grids are often set up on true north (with numbers on the X axis increasing toward the east and numbers on the Y axis increasing toward the north), but this is not always the case; site topography or other circumstances can dictate the grid orientation. If the site has been excavated before, you may want to orient the grid with the previous excavation to make correlation of units and deposits easier. The orientation of the grid influences the orientation of the excavation units (and vice versa), as excavation units are usually lined up with the grid. The grid serves as a basis for mapping, and the datum of each excavation unit can be tied directly into the grid. It also defines the location and size of your excavation units. Grid size will vary according to topography, vegetation, overall size of the site, and research needs, but the most common grid sizes are 1×1-, 2×2-, 5×5-, and 10×10-m units.

The grid can be set up using a compass, tape, and wooden stakes or nails, but for greater accuracy it should be established using an instrument such as a transit or theodolite. It may not be necessary to physically set up a grid using stakes or nails, especially if you are using a theodolite to map the site (see Chapter 7). For example, at Combe-Capelle we set up our excavation units off of Ami's original trench and mapped all material using a laser theodolite with an electronic distance meter. Because we did not need an actual grid for unit location or for mapping purposes, we didn't set up grid stakes on the site.

EXCAVATION UNITS

Your choice of excavation units will be based on several factors. One of the most important factor is whether you want to emphasize vertical or horizontal excavation. Vertical excavation, which focuses on exposing buried deposits at a site, is used to obtain information on chronology, stratigraphy, and artifact assemblage sequences. Horizontal or block excavations are used to open up a large area to examine the relationships of features and artifacts within a site. Horizontal excavation provides more information on one specific time period and allows you to address site structure and organization.

Your choice of excavation units will also be based on the topography and vegetation on your site, the depth and nature of the deposits at the site (for example, are they sand or clay?), and the type of site you are excavating (for example, is it a Paleolithic site or a prehistoric village?).

Your ultimate goal should be to choose excavation units that will maximize the amount of information you can obtain from a site. You may also use several different types of units to ensure recovery of a representative sample of material at the site. The following sections describe the most common types of excavation unit.

Test Pits

Test pits include soil augers or cores, shovel tests (several turns of a shovel), and 1×1-m units excavated to determine the presence, nature, and depth of deposits; to identify site boundaries; to locate and identify the types of artifacts and features on a site; and to define the stratigraphy of a site. Test pits may also be excavated within features to evaluate feature composition and function. Test pits are often used to help determine if additional excavation is warranted.

- Advantages: Test pits provide some preliminary information on archaeological remains at a site.

- Disadvantages: They require additional excavation to fully document the nature of the archaeological remains; test units are usually used as a first step in making decisions for full-scale excavation.

Setting up an excavation unit

Trenches

Trenches are long, narrow excavation units. Trenching is used to view stratigraphy, to collect a sample of artifacts for chronology building, to locate features, and to determine site boundaries. There are four different types of trenches:

1. *Slit trenches* are used to provide a vertical exposure; they are the most common trench type and range in width and depth depending on the nature of the deposits.

2. *Step trenches* are long trenches whose depth is stepped as you go down; they are often used to excavate mounds or deeply buried deposits. They provide a good view of the stratigraphy at a site. Wider step trenches can be excavated to provide a larger sample of artifacts and features.

3. *Backhoe trenches* are often used to identify subsurface deposits and features when surface visibility is low or when time constraints limit the use of hand-dug trenches. Because backhoe trenching can be destructive, you need to weigh its use against your data and time needs.

4. *Wall trenches* are excavated next to architectural features to outline the walls.

   - Advantages: Trenching provides good vertical exposure (time depth), helps locate buried features, and provides a sample of artifacts for chronology building and interpreting site function.
   - Disadvantages: Trenching can be destructive. Although hand digging gives you more control than does backhoe trenching, you can still damage archaeological remains. Because trenching does not give you broad exposure, it is difficult to define activity areas, determine site structure, or address the relationships of artifacts and features. Trenching can also be extremely dangerous, and the collapse of walls in deep trenches has resulted in some deaths. If you are excavating deep trenches, you need to be careful to shore up the walls or use a step trenching technique.

Squares

The most common excavation squares used in Old World archaeology are 1×1-, 2×2-, or 5×5-m squares; however, the size of unit you choose depends on what you want to recover and the degree of exposure you need. Contiguous squares can be used for block excavation to open a large area. Excavation squares are usually tied into the site grid and are measured from the PSD. Each square is also given its own datum point, and material recovered in the square is mapped using that datum.

- Advantages: Squares provide good control of provenience and give you relatively good area exposure, especially if the "edge effect" is taken into account. This effect occurs because material that is essentially in adjacent squares may extend into the square you are excavating.
- Disadvantages: Because of their often limited size, squares typically don't provide the vertical exposure that you can get with trenches.

Features

A feature is a nonportable artifact that cannot be removed from its matrix without destroying its integrity (Sharer and Ashmore 1993:613). Some of the most common features recovered at archaeological sites include firepits, postholes, caches, burials, pits, and structures. Features may serve as excavation units; the borders of the feature serve as the unit border. If the feature is used as the unit, it can be excavated entirely, sectioned (excavated in halves) or quartered (excavated in quadrants, or quarters). Digging in halves or quarters will expose vertical faces to help define the stratigraphy within the feature, will allow for detailed recording, and will provide more control over unexcavated areas. Features are often tied into the site grid for provenience and mapping purposes. If there is a lot of overburden (more recent and sterile sediments overlying the occupation surface) on a site, you may strip the surface to expose features. This is often done with a front-end loader or backhoe blade, and the features are then excavated as units.

- Advantages: Excavating features ensures the recovery of data on site function and provides information on the range of activities performed at the site.
- Disadvantages: If you rely only on data from features, your results may be biased. Often areas between formal features served as important activity areas at a site, and these areas may be ignored if you focus on features. Trash deposits also yield significant information about a site, and these deposits may not be excavated if they don't occur as formal trash pits.

UNIT PLACEMENT

In addition to choosing the types of units you will use during an excavation project, you also need to decide where to put them. Although you may decide where you are going to put your units when you set up a project, you need to remain flexible. Often you will change your unit locations as you excavate and find out more about a site.

Unit placement will depend on many of the same factors involved in choosing the types of units you will use. In deciding where to place your units, you should consider several factors.

Research Goals

In considering your research goals, you should think about the following questions: What is it that you want to learn from the site? Where are deposits that are most likely to answer your research questions?

Sampling Strategy

Because it is rarely possible to fully excavate a site, all excavation involves some kind of sampling. The type of sample you choose will depend on your research questions and the data you need to answer these questions. Your sampling strategy will often determine where you place your excavation units and the types of excavation units you choose.

- *Judgmental (nonprobabilistic) samples* involve placing units using some prior knowledge of the site. Often archaeologists use surface data to guide their unit placement. Units are placed in deposits that are most likely to provide information that will help answer research questions. We used this sampling strategy at Combe-Capelle.

- *Probabilistic samples* are based on mathematical probability theory, and sampling is done to obtain a controlled, statistically valid portion of a population (in this case, the site) that can be used to make inferences about the population as a whole. Your sample units, which are divisions of the sample universe you select to represent the population, are your excavation units. Several kinds of probabilistic samples can be used when you excavate a site. Two of the most common sampling strategies used in excavation are random samples and stratified random samples.

  Random samples involve defining sample units such as 2×2-m squares over the entire site and using a random numbers table to select the units to excavate. Each unit therefore has an equal chance of being selected.

  Stratified random samples involve using previous knowledge of the site to divide the population (site) into subpopulations that are similar. Random samples are then taken within these subpopulations. For example, you may take random samples within different areas of a site such as trash areas, architectural features, and artifact concentrations.

Site Topography

Contour lines on site maps illustrate the site topography and will help you in choosing the size and location of your excavation units. You should determine the size of the contours represented by the contour lines and look at the distance between contours; closely spaced contour lines indicate a steep slope, whereas widely spaced contours indicate a flatter surface.

Site Vegetation

If your site is covered with dense vegetation, you may have to place your units in areas where vegetation is less dense. Vegetation can sometimes provide clues to the nature of the subsurface deposits.

Deposit Depth

You need to consider the likely depth of deposits when you place your units; for example, you wouldn't want to put a unit in an area that has experienced a great deal of erosion or where bedrock is exposed.

Placing your backdirt is also a consideration when placing your excavation units. It is always tempting to put the backdirt pile near the excavation units, but this isn't always possible or advantageous, especially if you are doing block excavations or need to expand your excavation units. In these cases, a screening station can be set up away from the excavation units, and sediment can be transported there using buckets or wheelbarrows. It is also important to report on the position of your backdirt pile so that other archaeologists will know its location.

UNIT DEFINITION AND PLACEMENT AT COMBE-CAPELLE

At Combe-Capelle our goal was to find the limits of Ami's trench and to set up units next to his trench to obtain a good sample of artifacts from each stratigraphic level that he excavated. Because his trench was so large, we wanted to sample the upper, middle, and lower portions to ensure that we obtained a representative sample of material from the entire trench.

One of the biggest challenges initially was the fact that Ami's trench was badly overgrown and had slumped in over time. This made it difficult to define the original trench boundaries. We had to locate the original trench before we could place our excavation units next to it. We started in the center of the trench and worked outward until we found the edges, removing the backdirt from his excavation and dry screening it through 1/4-in mesh screen. Most of the initial season at Combe-Capelle was spent doing this. Fortunately the backdirt was much looser than the intact layers, so it was relatively easy to discern the contact between the two.

After the old backdirt was cleared to expose the western outline of the trench, we set up a trench (Sector II) perpendicular to Ami's trench, running west from its edge. We excavated this sector to correlate with Ami's stratigraphic levels. In this sector, we excavated 1 × 1-m units along the trench face. These squares were distinguished by a letter (X axis) and a number (Y axis) that showed their location relative to the PSD (for example, L1015). These units were tied into the PSD using the theodolite.

Two units were excavated at the base of the hill slope in what we called Sector I to sample the lower portion of the trench and obtain a sample of material to examine raw material use at the site. Here we did not use traditional squares but rather defined the units as rectangles. Unit A1 was excavated at the base of Ami's trench and was 2 × 1.5 m. Unit A2 was excavated adjacent to the west side of his trench to expose the stratigraphic sequence and was 4 × 2.5 m in size.

Sector III was excavated toward the top of Ami's trench, in an area where bifaces and Upper Paleolithic tools were recovered during the initial excavations at Combe-Capelle, to determine if a Mousterian of the Acheulian Tradition (MTA) industry was present there. Two units were excavated adjacent to the east side of Ami's trench. Unit C1 was 2×2 m in size, whereas D1, which was adjacent to C1 (downslope), was 3×1 m.

As you can see, our unit placement was chosen to answer our research questions. The size of the units varied because we were point proveniencing and using a theodolite for mapping, which meant that the use of standardized excavation units was not necessary.

OVERVIEW OF THE UNIT DEFINITION SCREEN

Before defining units for your own virtual project, start the *Virtual Dig* software and choose the **File/Use Real Combe-Capelle Data** option. To see the units that were originally defined for Combe-Capelle, choose the **Setup/Place Excavation Units** option. The window that comes up shows a contour map of the site and the outlines of Ami's original trench. In the lower left-hand corner of the map is the PSD, which has been given the coordinates 0, 0. In this grid the Y axis points straight up the hill (which is close to, but not exactly, north). If you move your mouse around the map, you will see the X and Y coordinates change, indicating their distances (in meters) from the PSD.

Superimposed on this map and outlined in purple are the various excavation units that we set up. The purple color indicates that these units have already been excavated (by us). If you click the mouse on any of the units, the name of the unit will be highlighted in the list at the left-hand side of the window. Alternatively, if you click on a unit name, the unit itself will be highlighted on the map. The status (new, in progress, or finished) is also indicated. Of course, for the real Combe-Capelle data the units are already finished.

For your virtual project, you must define a unit before you can dig it. The standard unit size for this program is a 1×1-m unit. To create a new unit in your project, hold down the left mouse button and drag the blue square (just left of the map) onto the map. When you let go of the mouse button, the square is dropped on the map as a new unit. Before you excavate a unit you can change its location by dragging it. You can choose as many units as you want and arrange them according to your needs. For example, you can make a trench by putting in a line of contiguous units or a 2×2-m unit by placing four units together. You can define new units at any time during the excavation of your virtual project.

New units are given a default name by the program. You can change the name of a unit or delete it but only if you have not started to excavate it.

Suggested Readings

Barker 1993; Hester, Shafer, and Feder 1997; Joukowsky 1980; Sharer and Ashmore 1993

EXERCISE 5.1

Learning the Unit Definition Screen

Set up a new file using the **File/New** option and give it whatever name you like. Then choose the **Setup/Place Excavation Units** option. Place a series of units that you would use to do the following:

1. Define the site boundaries
2. Excavate in deposits similar to Ami's to clarify the industrial sequence

Print the grid maps for both of these excavation strategies. Explain in the space below why you placed them where you did.

EXERCISE 5.2

Virtual Project

Now you are going to choose your units to answer the research questions you came up with for your virtual project. Think about what kinds of data you will need and, based on the previous discussion, what kinds of units you will need.

The first step is to set up the database for your virtual project, again with the **File/New** option. Remember, you will use this database file for your entire excavation, so be sure to give it a name that you will remember. To return to this file and continue your work in the future, use the **File/Open** option to reload your file. The current file name will always appear at the top of your screen.

Place the units you will use to excavate the site for your virtual project. Once you have decided where to place your units and are satisfied with your choices, close the window. The units you have defined will be saved, and your future decisions will be tied to the units you have chosen for excavation. Remember that you can create new units at any time, and you can always delete unexcavated units.

Excavation Methods and Artifact Recovery

6

EXCAVATION METHODS

After deciding what types of excavation units you will use and where they are to be placed, the next step is to determine the methods you will use to excavate them. In this chapter and the next, we cover the basics of artifact recovery. In this chapter we discuss the kinds of tools that are used during a typical excavation project. In Chapter 7 we discuss methods for proveniencing artifacts, as well as screening and its effect on artifact recovery. These are important considerations for any field project. When you are setting up a field project, it is imperative that you think carefully about these topics, their impact on the kinds of information you can recover, and the costs associated with them.

EXCAVATION TOOLS

Many different kinds of tools are used during an excavation project, ranging from backhoes to dental picks. Tools and other field equipment often form a significant portion of a field budget. They also have a major impact on what you will recover and the speed with which you recover it. You should consider the following factors when deciding what tools to use:

- *The nature of the deposits you are excavating.* For example, hard-packed clay is much more difficult to dig than fine silt, and you may need to use an ice pick or hand pick to remove material.

- *The nature of the archaeological remains on a site.* Fragile remains such as features or bone should be excavated carefully with a trowel or dental picks and small brushes to ensure that no information is lost. In contrast, trash fill can often be excavated with a shovel.

- *The excavation strategy.* You are more likely to use a shovel or even a backhoe to strip off dirt if you are doing block excavation, whereas you may use a trowel and other small tools if you are excavating a profile vertically.

Common excavation
tools used on a Paleo-
lithic site

- *The amount of time available for excavation.* Obviously you can remove more dirt more quickly with some tools than with others. However, when you opt for tools that can be used to excavate quickly, such as a shovel or a backhoe, you may lose some artifacts or information on their context.

The following is a list of tools that would be used on a typical excavation project:

- Long-handled pointed and square (snub)-nosed *shovels* are most commonly used. Pointed shovels are often used to loosen soil when digging; snub-nosed shovels are used to shovel-skim and clean walls.
- Pointed *trowels* are used for excavating, and square trowels are often used to clean walls.
- *Pick mattocks or hand picks* are used to loosen soil, especially hard-packed soils such as clay and caliche (calcium carbonate).
- *Heavy equipment* such as a backhoe for trenching or a front-end loader for stripping topsoil may be used in some instances.
- *Dental tools* are used for doing fine work such as excavating articulated bone or other fragile objects. Paint brushes are often used with dental picks for excavating fragile objects or features.
- *Tweezers* are used primarily for excavating fragile objects or taking samples such as charcoal for radiocarbon dates.
- *Ice picks* are useful for removing small or fragile material from hard-packed deposits.

Make sure that your tools are always carefully used and maintained; after the field season is over they should be cleaned, and broken tools should be replaced.

EXERCISE 6.1
Learning the Methods Screen

Open a new file and set up five units. Now click on **Set Excavation Methods** (or choose the **Setup/Set Excavation Methods** option) and click on the tab labeled **Excavation Tools.**

In the window that opens you are asked to estimate what percentage of time you plan to use various tools. You can change these estimates by moving the slider under each tool. As you move the percentage of use for one tool, the percentages for the other tools move automatically to ensure that you have accounted for 100% of your time. If you move a slider to 100, all the other tools will be set to 0. If you manually move a tool to 0, the percentage for that tool will not be adjusted automatically as you adjust other tools. Based on the number of units that you have defined, the program calculates how many people you will need to get the job done using those tools.

1. Compare in the spaces below the effects on your crew requirements and budget (shown on the bottom of the screen) based on these three choices:

   a. a shovel for 70% and trowel for 30%

   b. a dental pick for 70% and a trowel for 30%

   c. a backhoe for 70% and a handpick for for 30%

2. Describe in the space below an instance when you might choose to excavate with a dental pick instead of a shovel.

EXERCISE 6.2
Virtual Project

Open your virtual project file. Choose the **Setup/Set Excavation Methods** option, and click on the **Excavation Tools** tab. Based on the research questions you are asking and the units you have chosen, choose the tools you plan to use to excavate your virtual project. This is just an estimate of the tools you will use. During excavation you will have the opportunity to choose whatever tools you like at any time.

Mapping and Proveniencing 7

Archaeologists are not just interested in recovering artifacts and features for their own sake; they use these remains to talk about what happened at a site. Context, the location of an artifact or feature within deposits at a site and in relation to other artifacts and features, is what gives these artifacts and features their meaning and provides the basis for reconstructing past cultures.

In order to evaluate an artifact's context, archaeologists record its provenience, or three-dimensional location. The provenience provides the context of the artifact in terms of where it is located on a site and what deposits it is in. It also provides information on what other artifacts or features the artifact is associated with, which may help with interpretation of its use. For example, the interpretation of a projectile point will be quite different if it is recovered in the ribs of a mammoth versus in a burial. Provenience also lets you evaluate whether an artifact is in situ (in place) or has been altered or disturbed in some way. Provenience is thus one of the most important concepts in archaeology.

In setting up your field project, you must decide how you are going to record provenience. Your choice of proveniencing techniques will depend on the nature of the site you are excavating, the amount of material that needs to be provenienced, and the level of accuracy you require for the types of analyses you plan to do once you have collected the data.

DATUMS

Provenience is measured from the primary site datum (PSD), which serves as the central provenience point for the site. The PSD should be a permanent point on the site that can be found by other researchers if necessary, and the location of the PSD should be archived with the field documentation for the site. If all material cannot be mapped directly from the PSD, secondary datums can be set up (which are themselves linked directly to the PSD) and measurements then taken from them.

The PSD is assigned coordinates before mapping begins; these are called the X, Y, and Z coordinates or the northing, easting, and elevation, respectively. The datum coordinates are usually assigned arbitrarily, but the values should be high enough to encompass the full extent of the site so that you do not have negative values when you are mapping. For elevation readings, some archaeologists prefer to have the Z coordinate of the datum high enough to ensure positive readings, whereas others prefer to set the Z at zero so that depths are recorded as negative numbers. Still others measure elevation as centimeters below datum, which means that the Z coordinate would increase as you excavate.

The grid is set up relative to the PSD, and all grid coordinates are given relative to the PSD. Each excavation unit will also have its own datum, which is ultimately tied via the site grid to the PSD. Any of the unit corners (for example, NE, SW) can serve as the datum, but you should remain consistent in the corner you use for each unit datum.

METHODS FOR RECORDING PROVENIENCE

Manual Proveniencing

Manual proveniencing involves using measuring tapes to locate the material you are mapping (grid or excavation unit, artifact, or feature) relative to the PSD and recording the data by hand on graph paper. You can either measure directly from the PSD or use the excavation unit datum for your measurements.

If you are measuring from the PSD, one person will walk with a measuring tape from the PSD to the material being mapped to measure distance, while another person measures the bearing or angle from the PSD with a compass. For greater accuracy, you can use a Brunton compass, also known as a pocket transit. A Brunton can be used to map horizontal and vertical angles at a site; distance is measured with the tape. The Brunton can be either hand-held or, preferably, placed on a tripod, which gives it more stability and therefore greater accuracy. Bruntons can measure to within half a degree of accuracy without a tripod and are therefore more accurate than a traditional compass. With the angle and distance known, the X and Y coordinates can be computed trigonometrically.

For manual proveniencing within an excavation unit, measurements are often taken from the unit datum. Two methods can be used: (1) Use measuring tapes and a compass to measure north-south and east-west from the unit datum, or (2) triangulate from the unit datum to the point being mapped. Triangulation involves measuring angles to known, observable reference points such as grid or unit stakes and determining the location of the point you are mapping by plotting where the rays of the angles intersect.

Elevations can be taken using a line level and string or an instrument such as an engineer's transit. The line level and string should be placed at ground surface on your datum point so that all elevations are read below unit datum (BUD) and can be tied to the elevation of the PSD. To measure elevations using a line level, pull the string across the unit to the point you want to measure, place the line level in the center of the taut line and center the bubble within the level. Hold a tape measure vertically on the artifact or feature and read where the string crosses it to obtain your elevation BUD.

Manual proveniencing is reasonably accurate, but it takes considerably more time than does the use of instruments, and it does not offer the same level of precision. For this reason, most artifacts that are mapped manually are given only one provenience coordinate set (X, Y, Z) each.

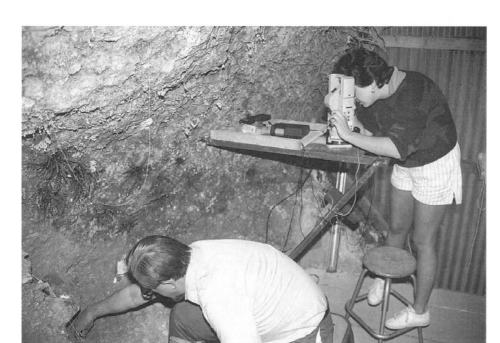

Using an EDM

Instrument Maps

Often you will desire or require a greater degree of accuracy for recording provenience than can be obtained with manual mapping, or you may have a large quantity of material that would be extremely time consuming to provenience using manual techniques. In these cases, instruments can be used to map the site. The two instruments most commonly used to provenience artifacts are (1) an engineer's transit and (2) a laser theodolite with an electronic distance meter (EDM). The instruments can be used to lay out and record the provenience of site grids and excavation units and for mapping artifacts, features, and other material at the site.

A transit is a surveyor's instrument that is set up over the PSD or a secondary datum. A stadia rod (which is graduated by height) is then placed over the point to be mapped, and vertical and horizontal angles and distance are measured by reading the stadia rod. The readings are recorded in a notebook, and the site map can then be drawn using these coordinates.

A laser theodolite with an EDM provides the most accurate and rapid means of recording provenience. The theodolite emits a laser that bounces off a prism mirror of known height that is set up on the point that you want to map. The laser returns to the machine and is used to measure the distance between the machine and the mirror, while the theodolite records the vertical and horizontal angles of that point in relation to the location of the EDM. After adjusting for the height of the prism, the theodolite calculates the three-dimensional location of the artifact relative to the PSD. It provides an accuracy level of ±2 mm, and a point can be mapped in approximately five seconds (Dibble 1987).

Points mapped with the theodolite can be written by hand in a recording book, or the theodolite can be linked directly to a portable computer. The computer operator can enter a code for the point being mapped (for example, F for flake, R for retouched piece), and the computer records the data for this material. It can also assign a unique identifier to the point. If the computer is linked to a small printer, you can print out tags to put with the artifacts as they are being excavated. The use of the computer system generates data that are immediately accessible in computerized format, and it eliminates data entry by hand, greatly reducing the chance of typographic errors.

In spite of these many advantages, the use of a theodolite involves a larger initial expense and you will need to have someone to run it during the excavation project. If you open up several units that are separated on the site, you may need more than one theodolite. However, for a long-term project, the speed and amount of information that you can obtain by using a theodolite makes it worth the extra expense. The computerized data obtained from mapping with the theodolite is also easily converted into other mapping applications such as Geographic Information Systems.

RECORDING PROVENIENCE DURING EXCAVATION

There are two basic ways to record provenience during excavation: (1) point proveniencing or (2) bulk proveniencing (also called lots). Because these procedures for recording provenience determine what can be done with the data once they are collected, you must think carefully about what kinds of data you need and how you want to analyze them before you decide if you will point provenience or use lots. Your choice will depend on the level of provenience control you need in order to answer your research questions, the amount of available time, and the available mapping technology.

Point Proveniencing

Point proveniencing each artifact recovered during excavation gives you the most control over your data because you know where each artifact was recovered and can carefully examine its context and association. It is especially important to point provenience if your site has complex stratigraphy and your research questions focus on stratigraphic relationships, as ours did at Combe-Capelle. In fact, almost all Paleolithic researchers point provenience each artifact because of the complexity of the archaeological deposits they are excavating and the importance of obtaining good information on the context of the remains.

Point proveniencing also allows you to do much more detailed analyses than does bulk proveniencing. If you have point provenienced all the material, you can aggregate the data during the analysis phase of the project; however, you cannot disaggregate material that was collected in a larger lot, such as a unit level. If you are using a theodolite, you can take provenience measurements on more than one point of the artifact. This enables you to draw accurate outlines of larger artifacts and features, and by measuring both ends of an elongated artifact, you can study artifact orientations (see Chapter 20).

Bulk Proveniencing

Bulk proveniences, or lots, are spatially defined units for recording provenience. The most common lot is the unit level, in which all artifacts within an excavation unit and from the same level are collected and analyzed together. The level can be either a natural stratigraphic level or an arbitrary level (for example, 10 or 20 cm). Lots are given a bulk provenience designation using the unit and level number (for example, Unit 4, Level 3) and are tied into the PSD via the unit datum. Often different artifact classes such as ceramics, stone tools, and ground stone from one level will be bagged separately, but they are given the same provenience designation.

For more fine-grained analyses, the excavation unit can be broken down into smaller provenience units. For example, a 2 × 2-m unit may be excavated in quadrants, or quarter squares, and each quadrant can be given a separate provenience designation. Excavating in quadrants can be confusing because the logistics of maintaining separate bags for each quadrant can be difficult.

Feature fill can also serve as a lot. Depending on the type of feature you are excavating, all the fill can be designated as one lot, or stratigraphic or arbitrary levels within the feature can serve as separate lots. This method ensures that all material from a feature is analyzed together.

In some cases it is useful to combine the two units of analysis; for example, you may use lots for lithic debitage (unutilized or waste flakes) but point provenience all stone tools. Tools are often point provenienced because of their potential to identify the kinds of activities performed at a site. In North American archaeology, it is common to use lots for most ceramic potsherds and lithic debris and to use point proveniencing for diagnostic (or time-sensitive) artifacts such as projectile points, other tools, whole or nearly complete ceramic vessels, and material in features.

SCREENING

Another important decision you will make about artifact recovery is what deposits you will screen and how you will screen them. Excavated sediment is screened to recover material that is not observed and collected during excavation. Screening ensures the recovery of small items, such as small flakes and pieces of bone, that can provide a great deal of information on the occupation of a site but that would be missed if only larger materials were collected. For example, small flakes removed from a tool during manufacture may indicate that a tool was made or repaired at a site, even if the tool itself is not recovered. Small bones, such as fish bones, can provide a more complete picture of a group's diet. Your decision on what to screen, what not to screen, and what size of screen you use will have a significant impact on the kinds of data you recover.

In general, all sediment from intact archaeological deposits should be screened, and material from critical contexts such as features is always screened. In some cases, overburden or sterile fill is not screened. Occasionally, if extensive deposits of trash or cultural fill are present, a sample of the fill is screened. Although it is preferable to screen all fill, screening is time consuming; and sorting screened material, especially if small screen sizes are used, is labor intensive.

The smaller the screen size, the longer it takes to screen and sort the material. As a result, the choice of screen size will be dictated by the data you need in order to answer your research questions and by time constraints. The standard screen size for archaeological recovery is 1/4-in mesh, which is used to screen most cultural fill. Smaller screen sizes (1/8-in and 1/16-in) are sometimes used for features such as houses, trash middens, and cooking pits. You may also use different screen sizes within one unit. For example, a quarter of a 2 × 2-m unit could be

Dry screening
sediments

screened through 1/8-in mesh while the remainder of the unit is screened through 1/4-in mesh.

The method you use to screen the material will also depend on the type of sediment. If you have loose, dry sediments such as silts or loams that pass easily through a screen, dry screening is the most common practice. The sediment is placed directly into the screen, the screen is shaken, and dirt passes through, leaving behind rocks, artifacts, and other material that must be sorted. If the matrix has large amounts of clay or is very moist, then wet screening is recommended. This is accomplished by using a hose, buckets of water, or stream flow to wash the sediments through a screen; the remaining material is then dried and sorted. Wet screening is more expensive, both because of the more complicated setup and because you have to factor in drying time, but it often results in much better recovery.

ARTIFACT RECOVERY AND PROVENIENCING AT COMBE-CAPELLE

At Combe-Capelle, all recovered material (flakes, tools, bones) over 3 cm in size and all rocks larger than a fist were point provenienced to geological level using a three-dimensional Cartesian system. We point provenienced all artifacts for two main reasons:

1. It was crucial that we maintain control over provenience information because of the complexity of the stratigraphy at the site and because one of our research questions involved examining artifact assemblages within stratigraphic levels. At times during excavation, it was difficult to determine the

stratigraphic level that we were digging in; the stratigraphy was apparent only after the level had been excavated. If we had bagged artifacts only by level, we might have placed artifacts that did not belong together in one level bag. Point proveniencing ensured that this did not happen. We were able to change stratigraphic levels when we needed to simply by changing the level designation for the individual artifacts based on their exact X, Y, and Z positions.

2. Point proveniencing allowed us to address the amount of postdepositional disturbance to the deposits by examining artifact orientations. Elongated or large artifacts or those with clear linear axes were mapped using two or more points. This provided information on their horizontal and vertical orientations and helped us determine if they had been moved substantially (you will use these data later in looking at the site taphonomy). We could not have done this if we had bagged the artifacts by level. The locations of rocks that were point provenienced were also helpful in addressing the geological processes operating on the site.

One of the main reasons we were able to point provenience all of the material and still excavate a major portion of the site was because we used a laser theodolite to record provenience. Manual mapping is a much slower process, and had we hand mapped all the material we would not have been able to accomplish nearly as much as we did. Although the laser theodolite was more expensive than hand mapping in the initial outlay, it was well worth it in the long run, given the data we were able to recover.

Small finds (small flakes and bone less than 3 cm in size) were an important data set at Combe-Capelle because they provided additional information on depositional processes at the site. We developed a method for using buckets as lots (bulk proveniences) to provide provenience data for these small finds. During excavation, excavators would fill a 7-liter bucket (about 2 gal), which usually represented about one-tenth of a square meter in terms of excavated surface area. The center of the area where we used the bucket for excavation was mapped using the laser theodolite, giving a provenience designation to the sediment and small finds within the bucket.

These buckets of sediment were then transported to a wet-screening station at the lab, where a hose was used to wash all sediment. All material was screened through 1-cm mesh screen at the wet-screening station. Nearly half of the sediment was screened through a nested screen system, first through 1-cm mesh and then through 2.5-mm mesh. After the sediment was washed with the hose, the material from the 1-cm mesh was placed in a drying tray with a provenience tag marked "coarse," and the material from the 2.5-mm mesh was placed in a drying tray with a provenience tag marked "fine." The small flakes and bones recovered from each screen were bagged with the provenience information of the bucket; therefore, the buckets served as lots. If material larger than 3 cm was found during screening, the artifacts were given a separate number, assigned the provenience of the bucket, and included in the analysis of the other artifacts that were point provenienced.

By using the bucket rather than a unit level as the lot, we were able to obtain closer control over the density of small finds per unit of sediment. The density of the cultural deposits was an important consideration in determining the degree of disturbance at the site, and this level of control contributed significantly to our ability to answer this question. If you want to do density calculations or volumetric studies (for example, determining the number of cultural items per amount of sediment), choose lots that will allow you to make accurate calculations. The "bucket shot" is one way of doing this.

During the third full field season at Combe-Capelle, we decided to stop screening material through the finer 2.5-mm mesh screen. We felt that fine screening was not worth the effort for the amount of information we were getting. The finer fraction took longer to dry and much longer to sort through than the coarse fraction, and we had already obtained a large sample of material from fine screening done up to that point. This illustrates the importance of flexibility in the field. When we found that our screening strategy was no longer working, we changed strategies.

Suggested Readings

Dibble and McPherron 1989, 1997

EXERCISE 7.1

Virtual Project

We will explore some of the issues concerning point versus bulk proveniencing and screening in more detail in the Excavation module. At this point, however, you can choose the artifact recovery methods you will use for your virtual project. Open your virtual project file. Choose the **Setup/Set Excavation Methods** option, and click on the **Screening** tab. Decide if you will screen your deposits from your virtual project, the percentage that you will screen, and the type of screening you will do (wet or dry). You will be screening through 1-cm mesh screen, as we did at Combe-Capelle.

Now click on the **Mapping and Point Proveniencing** tab and choose your methods for recording artifact provenience. If you choose to use a theodolite, you can decide whether you want to rent the instrument or buy one. That decision depends on how many field seasons you plan to have.

Personnel

When setting up your field project, you need to evaluate how many crew and specialists you will need to successfully complete your project. You will do this by determining how much you want to excavate, how many days per week you will be in the field, and how many weeks you will spend there. You want to try to put together a group of people who will work hard and who will also work well together. All of these decisions will have a major impact on your project's success and on crew morale.

FIELD AND LAB CREW

Most field projects will have a certain number of crew that are organized in a project hierarchy. The following list describes the crew you would take on a typical excavation project:

- *Principal investigator/project director (PI/PD).* PI/PDs oversee and manage the project. They make sure the excavation strategy is consistent with the research goals, the budget is being spent correctly, and the crew is happy. Because they also oversee the laboratory and analysis portion of the project, they usually divide their time between the site and the lab. PI/PDs are also responsible for the final site report; they usually put it together with contributions by other crew. Most projects have one PI/PD, although in some cases, two or more co-directors work together. For your virtual project, you are the PI/PD.

- *Site supervisor/crew chief.* These individuals are responsible for the on-site excavation. They make sure that the units are set up and excavated correctly, that all the field documentation is filled out, and that the excavation runs smoothly. Because this can involve a great deal of work, you usually have a minimum of one site supervisor per 10 excavators. In addition to overall site supervisors, you may have square or unit supervisors who oversee several excavation units.

- *Lab supervisor.* The lab supervisor oversees all of the laboratory processing and analysis. This person is responsible for making sure that all

53

material from the field is returned to the lab with correct provenience information and is washed, labeled, sorted, and given to the proper analysts. The lab supervisor is usually responsible for arranging for the final storage (curation) of the artifacts.

- *Crew members.* Crew members are those who do the field and lab work. Field crew excavate the units and do other field-related activities. In general, you will need at least one crew member per 1 × 1-m unit. However, not all of your field crew will be excavating 100 percent of the time. If you are point proveniencing with a theodolite, one person will need to operate it. Other crew members may be setting up excavation units or mapping in units, which will take them away from actual excavation.

  Lab crew wash, label, and sort the artifacts once they are excavated and prepare them for analysis. They may also assist in the analysis and may help prepare the final report. In general, you should have one lab person for every three excavators, depending on the density of finds. Keep in mind that these numbers are general and will vary depending on the number and depth of the excavation units, the amount of material recovered from them, what kinds of tools you are using, and how many people can be supported by your field facilities. You also need to plan for contingencies. Crew members get sick, have family emergencies, or quit unexpectedly. These situations will affect your project, and you should build in some flexibility when planning your project. You want to avoid having too few or too many crew for the tasks you want to do.

- *Support crew.* In addition to your field and lab personnel, you may hire some individuals to work at the living site if you are living communally. These crew members would include cooks, cook's assistants, and house cleaners. The size of your field and lab crew will determine the need for and number of these individuals.

SPECIALISTS

Almost all archaeological projects are multidisciplinary endeavors in the sense that no archaeologist can be an expert at everything. It is therefore a common practice to hire specialists to work in the field with you or to analyze specific kinds of material recovered from a site. The specialists you need will depend on the type of site you are excavating and your research goals. For example, if you are excavating a Paleolithic site where large game was found, you would want to hire a faunal analyst to identify the animals that were eaten. Keep in mind that although some specialists must work in the field with you, others can visit the site periodically during the project, and others can stay in the lab and do the analysis once the material is excavated.

The following list describes some of the specialists you would hire for a field project:

- *Artifact analyst.* Artifact analysis is usually supervised by a specialist and is often done in the lab while fieldwork is going on. Two major classes of artifacts are recovered from archaeological sites: ceramics and lithics. Many archaeologists specialize in one or the other. Analysis of other types of artifacts, such as historic artifacts, metals, wood, and shell, may be needed depending on the type of site you are excavating. In some cases, artifacts are sent to an analyst after the fieldwork is done.

- *Geologist/geoarchaeologist.* These specialists help interpret the geological processes at a site to address how the site formed, the degree of site disturbance, and changes in the local environment over time. They use stratigraphic profiles to study different depositional layers at a site, the processes responsible for these deposits, and their environmental setting.

- *Computer specialist.* If your project is computerized, you may need to hire a computer specialist to oversee the computer system. This person is responsible for purchasing computer equipment, maintaining the equipment, and installing and monitoring the software used during a project.

- *Faunal analyst (zooarchaeologist).* Faunal analysts identify the animals recovered at a site and study the relationship between the animal remains and the occupants of the site, focusing on how the animals were used.

- *Ethnobotanist/palynologist.* Ethnobotanists identify plant remains, and palynologists identify pollen recovered from the sediments. These specialists use information on plants to get at subsistence practices and climatic change.

- *Skeletal biologist.* These specialists study human skeletal remains to address questions of demography (for example, population size, population composition, infant mortality), diet, growth and development, and disease.

- *Cartographer/draftsperson.* You may want someone to draw the final map of your site and any other maps and drawings (for example, profiles, feature plans, artifact illustrations) that you include in your final report. Computer cartography has become a specialty within archaeology, and it is common to hire a computer cartographer to produce your maps after the project is completed.

- *Photographer.* Photography is an essential component of field documentation, and it is important that you take good photographs during a field project. You may hire a professional photographer to come to the site periodically and take photos, or you may assign this task to a crew member who has experience in photography.

- *Dating specialist.* Dating samples are usually sent to specialists who work at labs where the samples can be dated. Charcoal for radiocarbon dating is collected during excavation and mailed to one of several labs across the world. Burned flint can be collected, along with the soil surrounding it, and sent to a lab for thermoluminescence dating. Samples can be taken from a hearth and sent to a lab for archaeomagnetic dating. In some cases, the dating specialist must visit the site. For example, if an archaeologist is unfamiliar with the method of taking archaeomagnetic samples, a specialist may be called to come and take the samples. If thermoluminescence dating is used, dosimeters must be placed in the soil surrounding the burned flint to get a reading on the background radiation in the soil, and often a dating specialist will place these instruments at the site.

BUDGET CONSIDERATIONS IN PLANNING PERSONNEL

In planning your project, you need to decide how you will fund your personnel and include this cost in your budget. Because personnel, including their travel and subsistence costs, usually make up the largest single component of your budget, you need to plan carefully.

You will need to decide if you will pay the salaries, travel expenses, and insurance for all, some, or none of your crew. Keep in mind the impact of these decisions on crew morale. Archaeology could not survive without the help of volunteers, but you cannot expect unpaid people to work seven days a week for six weeks without a significant decrease in productivity and morale. In contrast, paying a moderate-sized crew even minimum wage can be very expensive.

As with your crew, you need to decide how you are going to pay your specialists. Some specialists will require a salary and travel expenses, others may charge on a per-sample basis, and still others may provide their own funding. The charges will often depend on whether the analyst is in the field on a regular basis or is sent material to analyze. Some specialists will charge additional analysis costs once the analysis takes place. For example, a dating specialist may charge salary and travel expenses to take the samples and then charge for running the samples. These costs need to be negotiated with your specialists before you hire them.

PERSONNEL AT COMBE-CAPELLE

Our crew at Combe-Capelle consisted of two PI/PDs (one American and one French), one site supervisor, one lab supervisor, and a computer specialist who oversaw the computerized system we used at the site and in the lab. Lithic analysis was performed in the lab during the summer field seasons; this analysis was done by the lab director and one of the PI/PDs. The field and lab crew consisted of graduate and undergraduate students from French and American universities. Because of the main supervisors' responsibilities at the site, their travel costs were covered, although they were given no salaries. The other crew members were responsible for their own travel arrangements and were not paid salaries.

Several different specialists were used at Combe-Capelle. Two French geologists visited the site on a regular basis during excavation. They did not need any salary, but they required funding for some of the special analyses they performed. Geophysical analyses were performed by a specialist who required only room and board while he was on-site. There were also French faunal and palynological specialists who offered to work on those materials, but very little was recovered. The PI/PDs and site supervisor did the photography. The project also worked with a dating specialist, who required travel and room and board costs while she was at the site.

EXERCISE 8.1

Virtual Project

Open your virtual project file, and select the **Choose Personnel** option. Click on the **Crew** tab. Choose the crew that you will take on your project based on the factors discussed in this chapter. You need to decide how many crew members you will take; how many weeks you will work in the field; and if you will pay salary, airfare, or insurance for the crew. Keep in mind the effects of these decisions on your budget and on crew morale.

Now click on the **Specialists** tab and choose the type and number of analysts that you plan to use when you excavate Combe-Capelle.

There are the personnel you will have when you begin excavating your virtual project. Briefly discuss in the space below why you chose these particular analysts and why you didn't choose others. Also, explain your reasons for deciding what kinds of expenses you will pay for and the amount of salary you will pay.

Living Expenses, Equipment, and Supplies

9

Logistics present a major challenge in planning a field project. Two major logistical concerns arise in setting up a project: (1) living conditions (where you will live; how you will eat; transportation; and other personal needs such as laundry, banking, and mail) and (2) equipment and supplies. These are important issues that can have a significant impact on a project's success, and they need to be addressed carefully before you go out in the field.

LIVING EXPENSES

Living conditions have a major impact on a project's success because they affect crew morale more than most other aspects of a field project (with the possible exception of the weather). Because living expenses can be a significant portion of your project budget, it is sometimes tempting to cut corners to save money. You should be aware, however, that cutting costs too much, thereby resulting in difficult living conditions, may result in poor crew morale and reduce the amount of work that you can get done during a field season. Crew safety should also be a major concern when planning your living conditions. As PI/PD you need to make sure that your crew is taken care of well. You should thus carefully balance your decisions on living conditions to make sure that your crew is comfortable and well-fed but that you still maintain a reasonable budget.

Where to Live?

When considering this aspect of a project, you should determine if you will buy or rent facilities or camp. In addition to finding lodging for your crew, you will need to consider lodging for yourself (the PI/PD) and often you will have to find facilities for the lab.

If you plan to camp, you need to find an adequate camp spot with access to clean water and facilities (toilets, showers). You will also need to decide if you will provide tents or if crew members will bring their own.

If you choose not to camp, several options are available. You can stay in a hotel; again, you will need to decide what quality of hotel you will stay in, as it will affect your budget. You may also opt to rent or buy a house or apartment(s).

Factors to consider when choosing among these options include the duration of the field project, access/distance to the site from your permanent facility, availability of housing, crew size, and budget.

Where to Eat?

Your decision on meals will depend on the same factors that influence living arrangements. One of the most common strategies is to hire a cook for the project. This should be done with care, as the cook can often make or break a project. If you hire a cook, you should have a kitchen (or camp kitchen) available to him or her. You should also determine where to get groceries and arrange for transportation for the cook. Arrangements should also be made for the cook to get to the site and to live either at the site or nearby; in some cases, cooks can be hired from a nearby town and come to your camp or house to cook. The biggest advantage of a cook is that the food will be more or less of consistent quality and the cook can effectively manage a food budget through careful planning. If the crew is large, you may need to hire a cook's assistant or plan on at least one of the crew serving as a cook's assistant (usually as a rotating assignment).

Communal cooking is also an option, where each crew member or a group of crew members is responsible for cooking meals on given nights. If communal cooking is practiced, it is still necessary to arrange for buying groceries; perhaps different crew members can be responsible for this each week. Surprisingly, this option is often more costly than hiring a cook, due in large part to the difficulty of planning meals (often people want to make their specialties, which may require expensive ingredients that aren't used to make other meals). Similarly, a cook generally uses leftovers in preparing meals, whereas crew members will make a whole new meal, resulting in wasted food.

You may also choose to eat in restaurants. This can be expensive and depends on the location of the project and proximity to restaurants. Often arrangements can be made for a restaurant to provide group meals. If you choose the restaurant option, you will need to decide if your crew will have all meals at the restaurant or just certain meals (for example, breakfast and dinner). If you opt for certain meals only, you will need to make arrangements for the meals not eaten at the restaurant.

A final strategy is to provide crew members with money (per diem) and let them provide their own meals. They may choose to eat in restaurants or cook their own meals, but the decision is left up to them.

Vehicles

Another logistical consideration is how you will get to the site every day. If you are camping near the site, you may be able to walk, but this is not always possible. If you have to drive to the site, you need to decide if you will rent or buy vehicles and determine the number of vehicles you will need. The decision to rent or buy will be based on the project location (especially if it is overseas), project duration, and budget. The types of vehicles you get will also be influenced by the terrain you will be covering. For example, in some areas it is necessary to have four-wheel drive vehicles to reach a site, whereas other sites can be reached on paved roads.

You will also need to make arrangements for transportation for the cook and perhaps for the lab personnel in case they need to purchase equipment or attend to other needs. At least one vehicle should be available for them to use, or perhaps they can share vehicles with the field crew.

Personal Effects

You should also consider how you and your crew are going to take care of personal activities such as getting or exchanging money, doing laundry, shopping for personal items, and going to the post office. This will often depend on the location of the site, proximity to town, and availability of transportation.

A related issue concerns how days off will be handled. Because you will be giving your crew time off, you need to determine in advance if they are to arrange their own transportation for days off, or if you will provide vehicles for them. If you provide the vehicles, you should include mileage in your budget and arrange to have additional drivers listed on the rental agreement and/or insurance policy.

EQUIPMENT AND SUPPLIES

Equipment and supplies are another major logistical concern when setting up a field project, in terms of the budget and in terms of getting the project done. You will need to determine your equipment requirements before starting fieldwork. This is especially important if you are going overseas or will be in an area without easy access to shopping facilities where you can purchase material that you forgot. You should plan what you will need to take for basic field and lab equipment, mapping equipment, and any specialized equipment (for example, computers, scales, calipers) that you will be using. You should also determine if you will need equipment and supplies for the living arrangements you have planned. For example, if you are hiring a cook and renting a building for the kitchen and lab, you will need to make sure that the building has a refrigerator and stove.

In addition to the excavation tools discussed in Chapter 6, common field supplies include buckets and wheelbarrows to transport dirt, whisk brooms and dustpans to brush away soil from artifacts or features, line levels, string, and tape measures (30-m, 15-m, and 3-m tapes) for doing manual proveniencing, hammers or mallets, and paper and plastic bags for artifacts and samples. A plumb bob is an essential item for mapping. A plumb bob hangs from a string, and the weight of it holds the string plumb, or vertical. It is used to center a mapping instrument or engineer's dumpy level over a datum, and it can be used for mapping within an excavation unit to ensure the exact location of a point-provenienced object beneath a measuring tape. Root cutters or machetes may be necessary if vegetation is dense or if you are working in an area that has a large number of roots. Nails or stakes are used for setting up the grid and excavation units; nails are also used for stratigraphic profiling.

In setting up your project, you need to decide if you will purchase the equipment before you go into the field (in which case, you will need to decide how to transport the equipment into the field) or if you will buy it when you get to the project area. If you do the latter, you should determine what you will do with the equipment once you have completed the project.

LIVING EXPENSES, EQUIPMENT, AND SUPPLIES AT COMBE-CAPELLE

As with any other field project, logistics were a major challenge at Combe-Capelle. Our central headquarters was in a large building located 2 km from a village called Beaumont. The building was leased from a local landowner whose home was adjacent to it. The building was originally part of an old forge (smithy), and when we first took over it had to be cleaned and remodeled to include a kitchen, dining area, directors' quarters, computer room, and lab. It also had one bathroom and shower; a second shower was located outside. The crew lived in tents in a large field outside the main building but used the dining area as a meeting and recreation area. Crew members were required to furnish their own camping supplies.

During the first season the crew was relatively small, and they ate dinners at a restaurant in Beaumont. It is common practice for the crew on excavation projects in France to eat in restaurants. During the remainder of the field project, when the crew was much larger, a cook was brought over from the United States. The cook shopped for food and prepared all meals. During the year when we had the largest crew, two crew members served as cook's assistants; this job rotated on a daily basis throughout the crew.

Because all of the directors and many crew members were from the United States, they flew to Paris and then either took a train to a town near the site or met in Paris and rode to the site in the project vehicles. Two vehicles were rented each field season. One was used by the cook, lab personnel, and director; the other was used in the field. Laundry, shopping, and mail were taken care of in Beaumont.

EXERCISE 9.1

Living Expenses

Open a new file, and choose the **Setup/Plan Living Expenses** option. Choose two different types of accommodations and food preparation. In the space below, discuss the advantages and disadvantages of each of your choices.

EXERCISE 9.2

Virtual Project

Open your virtual project file, and decide where your crew will sleep, where you (the PI/PD) will sleep, and where the lab will be. If the crew is camping, you need to decide if the project will pay for camping supplies.

Click on the **Food** tab. Decide if you will have communal cooking, hire a cook, or eat in restaurants. You will also need to decide on the quality of the food you will eat.

Click on the **Vehicles** tab. Decide how many vehicles you will need to transport your crew and any support crew (for example, the cook). You will also need to decide whether you will rent or buy the vehicles.

Choose the **Setup/Equipment and Supplies** option, and determine the kinds and quantities of supplies you will need for the field, lab, and living accommodations.

Remember that these decisions will have a major impact on your budget and also on crew morale!

Developing
a Field Budget

10

One of the most important aspects of running a field project is developing and overseeing the budget. The budget is developed based largely on what you set forth in your research design. The amount of fieldwork you will do, the length of time you will spend in the field, the size of the crew, and the types of analyses you will do determine how much money you will need to complete the project. When developing your budget, keep in mind that you will not always be able to do exactly what you want to do because you won't have the money for it. That is why careful planning is such a crucial part of setting up your field project.

The first thing you should do in developing your budget is determine who is going to fund the project. Because funding agencies have different requirements and give different amounts of money for varying amounts of time, it is essential that you establish the source of your funding so that you can tailor your budget to your audience. Funding can come from a variety of sources, both public and private. You can get funding from federal agencies such as the U.S. Forest Service or U.S. Bureau of Land Management if you are going to do work on their land. Private developers may also pay to have the archaeology done before they develop a parcel of land if they will be using federal funds in the development or if state, county, or city laws require them to do so. Funding for fieldwork can also be obtained from various granting agencies. For archaeology, the major granting agencies are the National Science Foundation, the Wenner-Gren Foundation for Anthropological Research, and the National Geographic Society; for Paleolithic archaeology, the Leakey Foundation is another important source of funding. Each of these granting agencies has different requirements; in general, they fund projects for a certain amount of money and for limited amounts of time. Universities are also a major source of funding for archaeological projects, and universities and museums sponsor many of the archaeological projects being done throughout the world today.

After you have determined who is going to fund your fieldwork, you need to develop a grant proposal and budget that you can justify to the funding source. When you submit your proposal, several other professional archaeologists will review it. Funding is scarce for archaeological fieldwork, and the process is competitive. Although the decision of whether to fund a project depends largely on the work's overall importance, the quality of the proposal itself, especially in terms of how well organized and how well thought out it is, has a major effect on the reviewers' recommendations. You can be assured that each reviewer will examine your budget carefully to see if your costs are justified.

When developing your budget, you should consider the following:

- *Project duration.* Determine the number of days per week you will be in the field (remember to consider crew morale here) and the number of weeks you will spend in the field each field season.

- *Project personnel.* Use the information in your research design to determine the size and type of field and lab crew you will need to complete the project. This will depend on how much time you are in the field, how many units you want to excavate, and what kinds of tools you are going to use. You will also need to determine which of the crew will receive a salary and how much.

- *Specialized analysts.* Include in your budget the cost of specialized analysis such as pollen, flotation, and faunal analysis and dating. You will usually pay the analysts for their time (salary) plus any additional costs for processing or running the samples. Choose specialists that are necessary for your project, and try to limit the time they have to spend at the site.

- *Food and accommodations.* You have planned for this aspect of your project when deciding on your living expenses. These budget items will include the costs of hiring a cook, purchasing food, or paying for restaurant meals, and the costs of putting up the crew in a hotel, renting or buying a house, or purchasing camping equipment. Morale is the biggest issue to consider when planning this portion of your budget.

- *Travel.* Travel can be a significant part of the budget. You will need to determine how you are going to get to the project area (for example, driving, flying) and whose travel you will pay for. Both crew and analysts' costs should be included in this portion of your budget.

- *Vehicles.* You also need to decide how you will get to and from the site each day and how many vehicles you will need to accomplish this. Rentals are better for short-term use, but purchasing may be more cost-effective if the project is going to last several years.

- *Equipment and supplies.* These items form a major portion of the budget. You should inventory the equipment you have available and determine if you will need to buy equipment or if you can rent or borrow it. Computers and mapping equipment should be included in this portion of your budget.

Even the best-planned excavation project will incur unexpected expenses. These can include costs associated with such things as losing a week of work because of rain, having to take a crew member to the hospital, or having to take important visitors to dinner. You will encounter these events as you use *Virtual Dig,* so don't be surprised.

Most projects will have a discrepancy at the end between the projected costs and actual costs. Your goal in developing and managing your budget is to minimize these differences. Occasionally you may have to go back to the funding agency to ask for more money. Usually when you do this you will have to provide justification and show that you have used the money you had wisely.

EXERCISE 10.1

Virtual Project

Open your virtual project file. Choose the **Setup/Submit Budget for Review** option. A spreadsheet will show your budget based on the choices you made in previous screens. The left-hand column of the spreadsheet contains the budget items (for example, salaries, food, accommodations), and the other columns contain a breakdown of costs. There is also a miscellaneous category to cover unexpected costs that occur during an excavation project.

Look at your budget and decide if you are satisfied with the amounts you have budgeted to cover costs. You can also go to the next screen and see a pie chart of your budget. The pie chart provides a visual breakdown of the percentage of the budget devoted to each of the budget categories. Pay particular attention to the contribution of salaries and living expenses to the budget. If you want to make any changes in your budget, make them now by going back to the other screens.

Once you are satisfied with your budget, click on the **Submit Budget to Granting Agency** button. Your budget will then be reviewed and given a rating and recommendation. Keep in mind that competition is tough, so that even a good rating will not guarantee success. If your proposal is not accepted, click on the **Reviewer's Comments** tab to read comments about what you need to do to make your proposal acceptable. Make these changes and submit the budget again.

Once you have a budget that is accepted, you are ready to go! During excavation, costs will be charged to your budget, and it is your job to stay within your budget even if you change your excavation methods as you go. Keep in mind that lowering costs may help you get the project past the reviewers, but it could affect your crew's morale and the amount of work you can get done.

Optional Exercise for Setting Up Your Virtual Project

Write a proposal to conduct excavations at Combe-Capelle. Your proposal should include the research questions you will address during excavation, a description of your excavation units and unit locations, the tools you will use, methods for proveniencing and screening, and the project personnel who will work on the project. Print a copy of your proposed budget to include with the proposal.

Overview of Excavation 11

N ow that you have set up your project and have an approved budget, it's time to start excavating! In this chapter and the next two, you will learn the basics of excavating a site, including stratigraphy, various forms of field documentation, proveniencing, and screening.

Exercises in these chapters are designed to help you understand some of the challenges you will face when excavating a site. Remember that the ultimate goal of archaeology is not to recover artifacts in and of themselves, but to use the artifacts and other remains to reconstruct past behavior. This process begins with thorough, sound excavation techniques and continues with the rigorous documentation of the excavated material and its context.

THE DAY-TO-DAY ROUTINE DURING AN EXCAVATION

After all the planning that you do to set up a field project, it's exciting when you can actually begin excavation. During a typical excavation project, the first thing you do when you get to the site is establish a primary site datum and set up your site grid. Next, you set up your excavation units. Once the units are set up, you are ready to start digging.

Usually at least one crew member is assigned to a particular unit; if you are digging larger units, you may have several people in one unit. If you are dry screening, you may have one person digging while a second person screens the material from the unit. If you are screening away from your units, you may put the dirt into buckets or a wheelbarrow and wait until they are full before you screen the material. The crew chief or site supervisor will come by the unit occasionally to check on your progress and answer any questions.

As you excavate, carefully monitor the sediment, looking for artifacts or evidence of features. As you find artifacts, either map them in (if you are point proveniencing) or place them in a bag labeled with the unit, level, and provenience information for the unit. Artifacts recovered from the screen are also placed in a bag labeled with the provenience information for the unit and level you are excavating.

Combe-Capelle during excavation

Look for any changes in texture, color, or moisture content in the sediment, because these mark level changes if you are following the natural stratigraphy. If you are digging in arbitrary levels, keep track of how deep you have dug and stop digging and close out the level at the end of a particular depth (usually 10 or 20 cm [4 or 8 in] for each level). During excavation, make notes in your field notebook, and at the end of each level, fill out the excavation forms and write in your notebook a description of what you found and the nature of the sediment. You should also draw a plan map (that is, a map as seen from above) of the material in your unit. When you reach bedrock or sterile sediment in a unit, draw the final profiles or sections (as seen from the side) of the stratigraphy.

If you find a feature such as a hearth, excavate the feature as a unit. All artifacts associated with the feature should be bagged separately from the other artifacts from the unit. Often you will screen the feature fill through smaller mesh screen and take samples such as pollen and faunal samples from the feature. Even if you are not point proveniencing, map and photograph each feature and fill out a feature form (described in Chapter 13).

As you excavate you need to be concerned with safety. Place your backdirt carefully so that your unit walls are not at risk for collapse. Never dig too deep without shoring up your walls in some way. A good rule of thumb is to keep the width of the unit at least twice the depth. Don't throw rocks out of your unit; place them carefully away from the unit walls. Also, be careful if you are moving rocks in a level; lift with your knees, not your back. Don't put your hand under a rock unless you have first checked to make sure there are no animals or insects under it! If you're using a shovel, don't leave your shovel with the blade up because, just like in the cartoons, someone could step on the blade and get hit in the head with the handle.

A number of factors will affect how much you enjoy your excavation project. One major factor is the weather. Make sure that you dress appropriately for the weather. Another factor is your fellow crew members. Excavation can get monotonous, especially if you aren't finding a lot of material. Having a fun crew can make it more enjoyable, and everyone should try to help out as much as possible.

STRATIGRAPHY

Stratigraphy is one of the most important and most frustrating aspects of excavation. Stratigraphy is defined as the interpretation of strata carried out by archaeologists. Strata are sequential layered deposits that are the result of both cultural and natural processes; these processes can be additive or subtractive. The archaeologist's goal is to determine the relationship between the human occupation and the strata at a site. Stratigraphy is vitally important for interpreting the context of the archaeological remains, for placing the remains in a temporal sequence, for reconstructing past climate, and for determining the geological processes responsible for the deposits at a site.

Because stratigraphy is so important in excavation, a number of ways have been developed to study and record strata that will provide archaeologists with the information they need to evaluate the relationship between strata and human behavior. Because stratigraphy can be very complex, it is often beneficial to have a geologist or geoarchaeologist (who specializes in the geology of archaeological sites) along to aid in understanding a site's stratigraphy.

The chronological interpretation of stratigraphy is based on the law of superposition. This law states that the lowest layers of strata are the oldest, and those above them are more recent. It allows archaeologists to use stratigraphy to talk about temporal sequences and changes in deposition, climate, and culture over time. For example, objects found in a particular layer are younger than objects found in underlying layers and are older than objects found in overlying ones. Objects coming from the same stratum are considered to be contemporaneous, at least in geological time.

Stratigraphy involves determining whether deposits are naturally or culturally derived. This is done by studying the basic characteristics of the geological sediments that make up the layers. Together, these sediments form what is known as a matrix, or the physical medium that surrounds, holds, and supports the archaeological material (Sharer and Ashmore 1993:125). Soils and sediments provide key information on the depositional history of a site.

Sediments are mineral, rock, and organic particles that are deposited as the result of natural processes or human activities. Natural processes responsible for sediment accumulation include aeolian (wind-blown), alluvial (stream-deposited), colluvial (gravity), or volcanic activity. Sediments are usually described in terms of their mineral content and the sizes of particles. Cultural activities such as mound building and trash dumping result in the deposition of culturally derived sediments.

Soils are composed of mineral and sometimes organic materials that are weathered and altered in place owing to vegetation growth. A soil thus represents a period of relatively stable conditions to allow time for soil development. Differences in soil types can be attributed to differences in vegetation, temperature, and precipitation.

A stratigraphic section
at the site at La Quina

The strata at a site are defined using the following physical properties:

- *Compaction.* Is the sediment compact or loose?
- *Grain size.* Grain size is often defined as fine grained or coarse grained. For more detail, a Wentworth scale is used to describe the grain size: gravel (<1 mm), very coarse sand (1–2 mm), coarse sand (.5–1 mm), medium sand (.25–.5 mm), fine sand (.10–.25 mm), very fine sand (.05–.10 mm), silt (.002–.05 mm), and clay (<.002 mm).
- *Texture.* Is the sediment sticky, crumbly, or gritty? Texture will vary based on the percentage of sand, clay, or silt in the sediment. For example, clay tends to be sticky, whereas sand is gritty.
- *Particle shape.* Are the sediment particles angular, subangular, subrounded, rounded, or tabular?
- *Color.* Sediment color varies based on iron, mineral, or organic content. Although some descriptions are limited to whether sediment is light or dark, a Munsell Color Chart is often used to describe the color. This chart has three variables: hue (relationship of a given soil color to yellow or red), value (a scale of lightness and darkness), and chroma (a scale of the intensity of the color).

In addition to the defined geological strata, you may observe lenses, or thin lines of deposit, within major geological beds. Lenses can be the result of natural processes or cultural activities (for example, trash deposition), and they can provide information about the depositional history of a site. They can also make it difficult to follow the natural stratigraphy.

Deposits at a site are also affected by various formation processes, which are cultural and natural processes that alter the context of artifacts and features. They can affect the form of an artifact, the spatial location of artifacts (so that things are not always found where they were used), the frequency of artifacts, and the association of artifacts and features. Cultural formation processes are cultural behaviors—such as picking up and using an artifact from an earlier site, digging a pit through older levels, or dumping trash—that alter the original context of an artifact. Natural formation processes such as wind, erosion, or animal digging can result in the mixing and movement of materials that will significantly alter their context. Studying stratigraphy can help you identify these processes and determine their impact on the deposits at a site.

Stratigraphy can be very useful for looking at postdepositional disturbance and assessing the degree of disturbance. The deposition rate, whether prolonged or rapid, will influence the types of archaeological remains recovered. If the deposition rate is rapid, preservation may be better than if deposition is slow; the longer organic materials are exposed, the more chance they have to decay. Various forms of erosion will also affect deposits on a site. Running water, deflation (wind erosion), and movement of sediments will remove deposits from a site and may redeposit them elsewhere. If the rate of flow is rapid, small artifacts may be transported, and large artifacts will remain. In Paleolithic sites, glacial movements were responsible for the movement of large segments of deposits. Repeated freezing and thawing may cause what is known as frost heave, in which deposits are pushed up. Large objects may also be pushed to the surface by repeated freeze-thaw action. Animal disturbance, especially rodent burrowing, may affect the integrity of deposits by mixing and introducing outside material. Even earthworms can significantly mix deposits. Roots are also a major cause of disturbance to stratigraphic deposits.

Cultural activities will also affect the integrity of strata. When people dig pits, deposit trash, bury their dead, or trample or plow a site, they disturb the deposits, which may affect the interpretation of the cultural remains recovered from them.

EXCAVATION STRATEGIES FOR RECORDING STRATA

Strata, or levels, are defined during excavation based on changes in texture, color, and moisture content in the sediment. Natural levels are excavated when the stratigraphy is clearly defined and can be followed during excavation. Unfortunately these levels are not always apparent until you finish excavating the unit and examine its profile. If you are bulk proveniencing, you may have to change the records for various levels to document the changes you observe in the stratigraphy.

Arbitrary levels are used as units of recording when you do not know the natural, geological stratigraphy or when it is not apparent. For example, you may dig in arbitrary 10-cm or 20-cm levels until you note sediment changes and can define the natural stratigraphy. Arbitrary levels may also be excavated within defined strata for increased provenience control if you are not point proveniencing. If you dig in arbitrary levels and are then able to define natural levels, you can combine material from several arbitrary levels once you determine that they are from the same natural level.

It is often useful to excavate a test unit when you start excavating a site in order to determine the stratigraphy. You may need to excavate several test units, as natural levels will often vary as you move across a site, and it is not always possible to correlate stratigraphy across a site. You should keep this in mind when developing your excavation strategy, because the stratigraphy in one part of a site may differ substantially from another. When excavating contiguous excavation units (squares), it is also a common practice to leave a baulk, or earth partition, to preserve the stratigraphy on the sides of the unit.

The best way to record stratigraphy is to draw a profile of the excavation walls. The walls should be vertical and cleaned from the top down with a trowel and brush prior to profiling. If you are using an EDM, you can record the level boundaries directly. Otherwise, a string with a line level on it (to make it level) is placed on the wall, usually on the top or somewhere near the center. A measuring tape is used to measure the depth of the deposits from the line, and these depths are recorded on graph paper. Generally the stratigraphy is drawn at some predetermined interval (for example, every 20 cm), depending on the complexity of the profile. The profile should include the major stratigraphic levels at the site, any lenses, and evidence of root or rodent disturbance. Always include a scale in your profiles.

EXCAVATION AT COMBE-CAPELLE

At Combe-Capelle we followed a typical excavation routine. First we set up the excavation units, and then the excavators began working. Each morning they would return to the same unit and continue to excavate in natural levels until they reached bedrock. We usually excavated with trowels and point provenienced all artifacts and other material over 3 cm in size and all rocks larger than a fist. We used a laser theodolite and EDM for the point proveniencing. We put the sediment into buckets and took it to the lab to be wet screened. Because the excavators were close together in the units, they had to be careful to avoid poking each other with trowels or putting their dirt in the wrong bucket! Excavators kept notes in a notebook for each unit, but most of the data were recorded on a computer attached to the EDM. One site supervisor stayed at the site all day, as did the French co-director. The American co-director divided his time between the site and the lab. The project geologists came out periodically to examine the stratigraphy and draw profiles. The field crew were usually a mix of French and American students, and they enjoyed working together and getting to know one another.

Because a major goal of our excavations was to expose the stratigraphic levels that Ami had excavated and obtain a sample of artifacts from them, we concentrated on vertical exposures. In Sector II, we excavated a trench parallel to Ami's trench that gave us both frontal (facing upslope) and sagittal (parallel to the slope) sections so that we could evaluate the stratigraphy in that part of the site. The units in Sector I were excavated to expose a sagittal section at the base of Ami's trench, and those in Sector III were excavated to expose a sagittal section at the top of his trench. The levels were defined during excavation based on changes in sediment texture, color, and grain size. These levels were numbered sequentially from top to bottom with numerals indicating major geological beds and letters used to signify subdivisions within them. A geologist visited the site on a regular basis to examine the exposed profiles and describe the geological processes responsible for the deposits.

In Sector I, we defined four major geological beds and a number of subdivisions within each bed. We identified four beds in Section II and two beds in Sector III. Because each sector was not linked directly to the others, the levels from each sector were given names preceded by the sector number (in roman numerals). Major geological beds were numbered sequentially from the top down with Arabic numerals, and smaller subdivisions within the beds were distinguished by letters. Thus there are levels I-1A, I-1B, and I-2A from Sector 1; levels II-1A, levels II-4A, and II-4E from Sector II; and levels III-1A and III-1B from Sector III. This means that levels I-1B and III-1B are not necessarily the same geological level.

The stratigraphy was not always apparent during excavation, and some beds were difficult to follow. Another problem was that rodent activity was present throughout the site, especially in Sector II, which made it difficult to determine the boundaries between certain levels. Excavators did the best they could, but the stratigraphy was so complex that at times excavators couldn't determine which level they were in while they were digging. Eventually the profiles helped to clarify the stratigraphy, and we were then able to use the computerized database to reassign level designations to material excavated from these deposits based on their original position.

Analysis of the stratigraphy at Combe-Capelle revealed that the beds represented a series of deposits laid down by different geological processes, with alluvial deposits in the lower beds of Sector I and slope deposits in the upper beds of Sector I and in Sectors II and III. One of the big problems that we focused on during the excavation concerned the degree of disturbance at the site. There was some evidence that the slope deposits had shifted via mass movement down the slope, but most evidence suggested that the degree of movement was not great. This problem, which we will return to in Part V (Analysis), illustrates the complexity and difficulty of interpreting a site's stratigraphy, especially in very old sites.

Suggested Readings

Drucker 1972; Gladfelter 1981; Harris 1975, 1989; Hassan 1978; Schiffer 1983, 1985, 1987; Wood and Johnson 1978

Excavation in *Virtual Dig* 12

EQUIPPING YOUR VIRTUAL PROJECT

When you set up your virtual project, you had to decide what field, lab, and living equipment to buy; if you would rent or buy a house; and what vehicles you would need to purchase. These were important considerations in developing your budget. Now that you have an approved budget, you need to purchase the equipment before you can begin excavating.

To do this, start *Virtual Dig* and open your virtual project file. Now go to the **Purchase Equipment and Supplies** screen under the **Excavation** menu or click on **Purchase Equipment and Supplies** on the main screen. This screen will show you the equipment and supplies you planned to purchase when you set up your project. You can make changes to this list now or go ahead and purchase everything that you originally planned. *Virtual Dig* will keep track of your budget. You can return to this screen at any time to make additional purchases.

Note that this screen is for making equipment and supply purchases only. Your other expenses (for example, food, travel, and salaries) will be deducted automatically from your budget at the start of each season. Remember that you cannot purchase equipment until your budget has been approved.

USING THE INTERACTIVE EXCAVATION SCREEN

During this part of the *Virtual Dig* you will be using the **Interactive Excavation** screen. Before we introduce the basic concepts of excavation, it is important that you become familiar with this screen.

Start *Virtual Dig* and open a new project file. Define one unit for excavation and leave all of the other setup items at their default values. You will also need to go to the **Purchase Equipment and Supplies** screen before you begin excavating.

Choose the **Interactive Excavation** option from the **Excavation** menu. The first screen that comes up shows you the units that have been defined for excavation. At this point you can add, delete, or rename units or change the locations of any of the units, as long as you have not started excavating. The screen shows you how much of your budget has been spent. As you dig, this value will increase. When your budget is used up, you will be allowed to continue excavation, but the actual expenses column on the **Budget Totals** (in the **Submit Budget for Review** screen) will reflect the fact that you have gone over your original budget.

To begin excavating, choose a unit to excavate either by clicking on the unit name in the box on the left or by clicking on one of the units on the map. Then click on the **Begin Excavating** button. Don't be surprised if you find out that something beyond your control has happened!

When you get to the **Excavation** screen, you will see in the upper left-hand corner a plan view (that is, looking down from above) of your unit. The first level is marked by green grass for the surface. As you dig, stratigraphic level changes will be apparent as sediment color changes, enabling you to excavate in natural stratigraphic levels. The upper middle portion of the screen shows you a profile view of what you have excavated.

To the right of the plan view are buttons for the tools that you purchased. If a tool that you want to use is not shown, you'll have to go back to the **Purchase Equipment and Supplies** screen and purchase it. You can select a different tool at any time, which gives you the flexibility you often need during an excavation project. A bigger tool will remove more dirt with a single scoop (which will make the excavation go faster), but it will also result in more artifacts ending up in the bucket with no provenience data. These artifacts can usually be recovered later if the bucket is screened, though if you use a backhoe, all of the artifacts will be lost.

Once you click on the tool you want to use, you excavate by moving the mouse over to the plan view and clicking anywhere within the unit outline. The square that appears corresponds to the size of the scoop that will be removed, but keep in mind that different tools can also dig deeper with each scoop. You make a scoop by clicking with the left mouse button, or you can drag the rectangle over the surface while holding down the button and continuously remove sediment.

As you dig, you will see artifacts appear as either circles, lines, or polygons in colors representing the types of artifacts they are (stone flakes, tools, cores, natural rocks, or animal bones). The shape of the object gives you an idea of its size, and the number of points making up an object represents the number of measurements taken on it during our excavation of Combe-Capelle.

As you move the mouse over the plan view, you will see the X, Y, and Z coordinates (as measured from the PSD) displayed. You can also keep track of where you are in the excavation unit by looking at the CMBS (centimeters below ground surface) counter.

After you have exposed some artifacts, you can point provenience them by clicking on either the EDM (if you have purchased or rented one) or the tape measure. Using the EDM allows you to retain the multiple measurements that were taken on many of the objects; if you use a tape, only one measurement will be taken for each object. If you do not want to point provenience, click on the **Clear Unit** button. This will bring the entire surface down to the same level, and any artifacts that are removed will end up in a bucket without provenience measurements.

Each scoop adds dirt to your bucket. Depending on how many buckets you have purchased you will eventually have to empty them in order to continue excavating. You can either screen them (and recover any artifacts that are there) or simply empty them into the backdirt. You do this by using the mouse to drag the buckets to the appropriate spot (either the screen or the dump), or you can use the left mouse button to automatically screen them or the right button to dump the buckets directly into the backdirt. Your budget will be charged more for screening because it takes longer.

On the right-hand side of your screen are some counters that will keep track of the last artifact identified in your level, the number of artifacts recovered through screening, and the number of artifacts lost (not recovered because you did not screen some buckets).

As you excavate, a profile will be created showing the levels you are exposing and their elevation (Z) relative to the PSD. Different colors will indicate different sediment types, and the profile view will show you the natural levels as you go down. When you see a color change, you should stop excavating in that spot and continue to remove the previous level from the rest of the square, measure in any exposed artifacts, and empty all of your buckets to make sure that any artifacts in them are provenienced within the correct level. Then click on the **New Level** button to define a new level.

USING THE AUTOMATIC EXCAVATION SCREEN

Because excavation is a slow process, we have designed a way for you to speed up the interactive excavation process using *Virtual Dig*. You can do this by going to the **Automatic Excavation** screen (under the **Excavation** menu). To learn about this screen, start a new project file and define one unit. Now go to the **Automatic Excavation** screen and choose the unit for excavation.

This screen looks similar to the **Interactive Excavation** screen. Before you excavate, choose the tools you want to use to excavate your unit (only tools you have purchased will be available). Your choice will affect the speed of the excavation, the rate of recovery (how many objects are mapped in, how many are recovered during screening, and how many are lost because you didn't screen), and your overall budget. Next, decide if you will excavate in arbitrary levels or in natural levels following the stratigraphy from another unit. If you are going to excavate in arbitrary levels, determine the depth of the arbitrary level. If you choose to use the stratigraphy from another unit, you will first have to dig a unit or units in stratigraphic levels using interactive excavation to generate the stratigraphic levels. Finally, you need to decide if you will point provenience (manually or using an EDM) and what percentage of the material you will screen.

Once you have chosen your methods, you can begin excavating by clicking the **Dig to Bedrock** button. Keep track of the Z as you excavate so that you know your current depth. Artifacts from each level will show up in the unit plan as you go, and a record of the material found in the screen will be created. An automatic profile will be created for each unit. You can click on the **Stop** button to stop the process at any time.

EXERCISE 12.1

Automatic Excavation

Start a new project file, and set up four units to excavate as you've done before. Skip the budgeting process and go directly to the **Excavation/Purchase Equipment and Supplies** screen. Click **Yes** to excavate with a default budget, and then click on the **Make Purchases** button. Now go to the **Excavation/Automatic Excavation** screen.

1. Excavate one unit to bedrock using a pick and shovel without screening (set percentage of buckets to 0).

2. Now excavate a second unit to bedrock and screen 100 percent of your buckets.

3. Excavate the remaining two units to bedrock using two different tools. For one unit, point provenience all material using the EDM. Screen 50 percent of your buckets. For the second unit, don't point provenience but screen all of your buckets. Save this file because you will use it again in Exercise 12.2.

Describe the results of your excavation of these units in the space below. Include information on the depth of the deposits, the number of artifacts recovered (hint: the number of artifacts recovered will equal the last ID number for that unit), and the number that were lost because you didn't screen. What are the advantages and disadvantages of the various methods you used?

EXERCISE 12.2

Automatic Excavation

Use the same file that you used for Exercise 12.1, and go to the **Automatic Excavation** screen from the **Excavation** menu. Place two new units next to the units you excavated previously.

Excavate one of these units using 10-cm arbitrary levels. Excavate the other unit with the same tool but with 20-cm intervals. Explain below the relationship between your arbitrary levels and the natural stratigraphy.

EXERCISE 12.3

Interactive Excavation

Using the same file that you used for the previous two exercises, go to the **Interactive Excavation** screen from the **Excavation** menu. Again place a unit in the same general area that you excavated earlier. Excavate this unit first with a trowel, then a hand pick, and then a shovel, point proveniencing objects and screening the buckets as you go. With each tool, note how many artifacts are turning up in the screen. Try to change to a new level with each change in soil color.

When you are finished, print the screen and compare the level designations you made with the stratigraphy defined using automatic excavation in the previous two exercises.

Field Documentation and Mapping

13

FIELD DOCUMENTATION

Field documentation, which consists of all of the records used to record data on your excavation project, is perhaps the most important part of an excavation project. As we discussed previously, excavation is destructive. Field forms, notes, and databases are therefore essential components of any excavation project because they provide the documentation needed to interpret the context of archaeological data recovered during the project. Adequate field documentation is also necessary to ensure that the data you collect can be used by other researchers in the future.

Most excavation projects have standard forms that are filled out in the field. Different projects use different kinds of forms depending on the nature of the site and the level of computerization of the project. Forms are generally filled out for each excavation unit or feature and become part of the documentation for the site. These forms ensure that the information you record for each excavation unit or level is consistent. Forms work well when you have clearly defined excavation units. If you are doing block excavation or excavating features that extend into several units, you may have to modify your forms to accurately document what you are excavating so that units and features can be correlated.

- *Excavation level forms* are filled out after each level is completed. These forms record the elevation of the level you are digging, the methods used to excavate the level, a description of the sediment and any changes in it, a description of the material recovered during excavation, and information on any samples taken.

- *Feature forms* are generally filled out after a feature is excavated and include detailed information on the feature, including contents, form, architecture (if appropriate), information on the matrix (sediment types), and samples taken from the feature.

In addition to this formal documentation, each fieldworker should keep a field notebook. Field notebooks can serve as backup documentation if the forms are lost or destroyed. They can also be used to clarify information and to supplement the forms. Daily entries should be made in the field notebooks. Information recorded in the field notebooks should include the unit, level, or feature you are working in; weather and light conditions (which affect visibility); whom you are working with; daily objectives; procedures (what is being done, how you are doing it); a description of the artifacts, features, and other material you encounter; sediment types; any changes in color, dampness, or artifact content in the unit; a discussion of the results of your work; and ideas about the interpretation and meanings of the finds. You are the one excavating this material, so you are the best person to discuss these things. Record *all* information, even negative information, as it may be an important clue. For example, saying that you didn't find any bone is better than just not mentioning it.

Field forms and field notebooks should be filled out in the field! This sounds like common sense, but when it is late in the day and you are hot or cold, tired, and hungry, it is often tempting to wait to work on your notes until you get home or until the next morning. You can lose a lot of important information if you do that, however, because you will forget many small details. It is imperative that you write notes in the field as you finish excavating a level or feature. Another basic tenet of field records is that if you question whether you should write it down, then write it down. In some cases this is the only record available for the project, so make it as thorough as possible.

DATABASES

During an excavation project, you generate a tremendous amount of data. Organizing and managing these data presents a challenge for archaeologists; therefore, the methods for recording data are an important part of the field documentation of a site. Because computers have had a major impact on the design and use of databases, we focus on computer databases in this discussion of field documentation.

The database you use should be set up at the beginning of a project, and it will guide the way data are collected. In designing your database, your goal is to organize the data into manageable units. A carefully designed database can help you find and eliminate errors in data collection and can determine what you are able to do during analysis.

If you are using computers to collect data for the whole project, you may have separate field and analytical data sets. Field data generally consist of provenience information for all material collected during excavation—including the X, Y, and Z coordinates; level; and the general kind of material you are proveniencing (for example, flakes, tools, bone). Analytical data include attributes you will look at as you study the artifacts; these attributes will be based on your research questions and the kinds of data available to answer them. For example, if you want to analyze provenience data or artifact orientations for all artifacts collected from a certain level at a site, you can do that only if the artifacts were mapped in individually. If they were collected in bulk proveniences (for example, by level), the data will not be available for that kind of analysis. This is why it is important to think about the kinds of analysis you want to do during the research design phase of the project, before fieldwork begins, to ensure that the methods you use are amenable to the types of analysis you want to do.

Your database will generally contain two basic kinds of data depending on what you are recording:

1. *Character attributes* such as level name, the general kind of artifact, and other qualitative observations
2. *Numeric attributes,* or quantitative measurements, such as X, Y, or Z and length or width of artifacts

For data entry, the analyst either enters data directly into the computer database or writes the data on coding sheets for later data entry. In the latter case, the chance of error is greater because of the extra step of having the data entered into the database. In terms of entering the data, some data entry or analysis programs work only with numeric data. If this is the case, you can convert character variables into numeric codes and follow a code sheet to keep track of the variables. Some data entry programs have menus that list the variables that can be chosen for a specific attribute. Menus tend to reduce error by avoiding problems with misspellings or typing errors.

Once you've entered the data, you should "clean" them (that is, check them for errors) before using them for analysis. Mistakes occur during data entry regardless of whether the data are hand-entered or computerized. Common errors include typos, misspellings, extra numbers, or misplaced decimal points. All data entry should be verified and errors corrected before the data are used. Because most of your work will be based on individual artifacts, the identification number can serve as the linking field. At Combe-Capelle we used the combination of unit name and ID number.

Databases can be linked so that data from each database (for example, field, lithics, fauna) can be put together into one large database when the final synthesis and interpretation is done. If you plan to do this, you need to identify a common field in the database that can be used to link them. In *Virtual Dig* we have only two databases: the field database, which contains provenience data on artifacts taken during excavation, and the stone tool database, which contains analytical data for the lithics.

The field database is built at the time of excavation. As each artifact is recovered it is assigned a unique ID number that, along with the X, Y, and Z coordinates and other information recorded at this time, is entered into the field database. Later, when further analysis is done on an artifact, the ID number is again entered as part of the stone tool database along with measurements and other observations taken on the piece. Because the same ID number is used in the field and stone tool databases, the provenience data of the first database can be matched easily with the analytical data in the second. Of course, this approach requires that each artifact be given a unique ID number and therefore that no duplicate numbers be assigned to separate objects.

ARCHIVING AND CURATING FIELD RECORDS

Even the best field documentation is useless if it is not properly archived so that it can be available to other researchers. All documents should be kept with the artifacts and other material remains recovered from the site. The documents provide the information necessary to place the material remains in context.

Written documents such as forms should be copied on acid-free paper when they are archived. Although computerized data can be stored on CD-ROM or computer disks, printed copies of the data (on acid-free paper) should be included with the documentation because the archival life of these computer technologies is not known but is most likely not more than 10–15 years, and rapid changes in computer hardware and software may render them obsolete relatively quickly.

FIELD DOCUMENTATION AT COMBE-CAPELLE

At Combe-Capelle, we did not use excavation forms, but each excavation unit in each sector had its own notebook. Excavators and the site supervisor would write in the notebook as they were working and at the end of each day. In using the notebooks during the analysis and write-up phase of this project, we found that there was incredible variability in the quality of the field records. Some excavators recorded detailed information on their units, whereas others left out important information. In retrospect it may have been better to combine the notebooks with a standardized form to ensure that the same basic information was recorded in a consistent way for each unit.

We relied primarily on computerized databases for our field documentation. We took steps to automate the data entry process to reduce the likelihood of error and to make the process easier. In the field the theodolite was linked directly to a laptop computer so that the X, Y, and Z coordinates were input directly. The person running the EDM input the level name, a code for the kind of artifact being recorded (for example, R for retouched tools, F for flakes, C for cores, and N for natural rocks), and the excavator's initials. The computer program automatically assigned the date and the artifact number, which was composed of the unit name and the ID number (a sequential number assigned to each object found in the unit). At the end of each day the field data were transferred to the main computer database in the lab.

The field computer was also connected to a small thermal printer that printed a paper tag for each artifact as it was being recorded. The tag contained all of the data for that artifact and was wrapped in foil with the artifact. The tag not only served as a backup in case the computer data were somehow lost but also indicated the ID number that was written on the artifact after it was washed.

We also recorded other excavated material in this manner. For example, we recorded all rocks larger than a fist, but instead of giving them a sequential ID number, we gave them an ID number consisting of a random set of five letters. The rocks were then discarded at the site. Once a bucket was filled with sediment, we took a "bucket shot" that provided the provenience of the fill in the bucket (see Chapter 7). These, too, were given five-letter ID numbers.

We conducted all analyses in the lab by entering data directly into laptop computers using special data entry programs. We created separate databases for each analyst, but these were later linked (or related) using the common fields of unit and ID number. We tailored each of these databases to the needs of the analyst and to the research questions. For any data that required measurements, we used electronic calipers linked directly to the laptop computers. We entered the measurements directly into the computer, avoiding many data entry errors. Periodically we transferred the data from the laptops to a central computer database where they were "cleaned" before statistical analysis was performed.

Because the data from Combe-Capelle were almost completely computerized from the beginning of the project, we were able to publish the data on CD-ROM as a companion to the written final report, along with close to 1,000 color images of the artifacts and pictures of the site during excavation (Dibble and McPherron 1989, 1997). The ease of publication and distribution is a definite advantage of

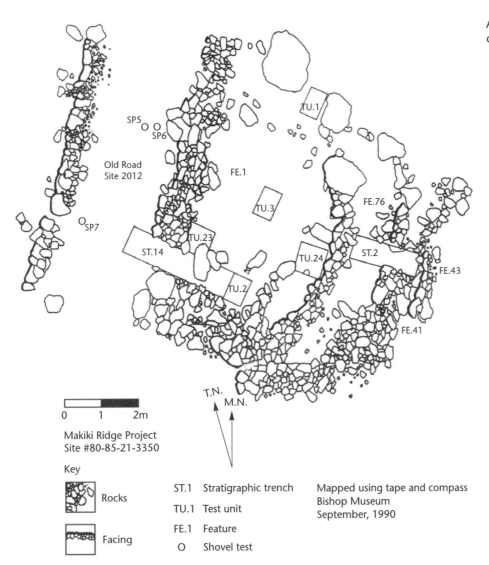

An example of a hand-drawn plan map

TU.1

SP5

SP6

Old Road Site 2012

FE.1

TU.3

FE.76

SP7

TU.23

ST.14

TU.24

ST.2

FE.43

TU.2

FE.41

T.N.

M.N.

0   1   2m

Makiki Ridge Project
Site #80-85-21-3350

Key

Rocks

Facing

ST.1   Stratigraphic trench

TU.1   Test unit

FE.1   Feature

O   Shovel test

Mapped using tape and compass
Bishop Museum
September, 1990

computerized databases. It is also the reason why *Virtual Dig* can be based on the actual data recovered from the site.

MAPPING

We have already discussed the importance of recording provenience information during excavation. Proveniencing provides the context of the artifacts and features you recover during excavation and helps you interpret what was going on at a site. Point proveniencing, where you provenience each artifact or piece of material that is recovered during excavation, provides you with more control over your data than does bulk proveniencing, where proveniences of individual artifacts are in relation to a larger area such as a unit level.

Provenience is illustrated in several different ways. If you are point proveniencing material by hand you will usually draw (or have a cartographer draw) maps of the provenienced material as it was found during excavation. If the provenience data are on a computer, then the computer can generate a map using various cartography programs. If you are bulk proveniencing, you will need to draw a map of the unit locations to show the provenience of the material.

Two kinds of maps are drawn for most excavation projects. Site maps are made to show the overall layout and distribution of material on the site. Site maps often include the site boundaries, major contours, landmarks, excavation unit locations, and any features or artifact clusters visible on the surface or recovered during excavation. When you put down your units in the **Place Excavation Units** screen, you created a site map.

Plan maps are created for excavation units, features, or in any other instance where you want to show the distribution and association of artifacts, features, and geological information. The figure on the previous page shows an example of the kind of patterning you can see in a plan map and illustrates what it can tell you about past activities.

In *Virtual Dig,* plan maps are displayed for each level in the field notebook, but you can also create your own plan maps and work with them interactively.

SCREENING

When you were setting up your project, we discussed the importance of screening material and the impact it has on artifact recovery. If you do not screen deposits, all information is lost unless you observe artifacts as they come out of the ground and point or bulk provenience them. Although it is not always necessary to screen all of the deposits at a site, you should at the very least screen a sample of the deposits, and all fill from critical contexts such as features should be screened. Screening can be time consuming, but the recovery of data is worth the effort.

Suggested Readings

Barker 1993; Dibble and McPherron 1989, 1997; Sharer and Ashmore 1993

EXERCISE 13.1

Site Notebook

Open a new project file, and prepare for excavation. Go to the **Excavation/Interactive Excavation** screen and excavate the unit using whatever methods you would like. The information on these units will be recorded in a notebook in the **Refer to Field Notes** screen under the **Excavation** menu. You can also access the notebook directly from the excavation screen by clicking on the notebook icon.

Open the notebook by clicking on its front cover. You will see a table of contents of the units that have been excavated. Clicking on any of these unit names will take you to the first page of the notebook that has information on that unit. You can browse the notebook one page at a time by clicking on the page numbers. Double-clicking on any page of the notebook will take you back to the table of contents.

Now fill out the Excavation Level Form on the next page for one level based on the information in your notebook and your experience with interactive excavation.

When you excavate your virtual project, you will need to look at your notebook to keep track of events that occur during the course of your excavation. This is especially true if you use the automatic excavation mode, because events can happen without you being informed of them.

Excavation Level Form

Site Number _____

Unit Number _____

Level/Stratum _____

Name _____

Date _____

1. Floor elevations (in cm) Beginning: Center _____ NW _____ NE _____ SW _____ SE _____

    End: Center _____ NW _____ NE _____ SW _____ SE _____

2. Notes (include methods, observations, problems, and a brief inventory of finds)

3. Nature of soil or fill (color, texture, and so forth)

4. Features (describe features in unit)

EXERCISE 13.2

Mapping

Open a new project file, and set up one excavation unit. Go to the **Interactive Excavation** screen, and excavate the unit using whatever methods you wish to use, but make sure that you point provenience all material. Now go to the **Plot Excavated Artifacts** screen under the **Excavation** menu.

In mapping, you can choose from your list of excavated levels or choose particular units. You can choose one unit or level simply by clicking on it, or choose several to map together by dragging the mouse over the list or by pressing **Ctrl** while clicking on several of them. If you choose one or more levels, all of the units that contain the levels will be displayed. If you choose a unit, all of the levels in that unit will be displayed. If you click on the **Plot** tab, the artifacts that have been excavated in a level will be displayed.

You can view the map from three different directions. An X-Y plot gives you a plan view (looking down on the unit from directly above). An X-Z plot gives you a frontal view (looking from the side in the grid-north direction). Finally, a Y-Z plot gives you a side, or sagittal, view (looking in the grid-west direction). You can color the artifacts either by level (which helps you to see the stratigraphy) or by artifact type. You can also zoom into a portion of the screen. Click on the **Reset Zoom** button to go back to the original scale.

When artifacts are shown on the map you can see the values of the two plotted coordinate axes as you move your mouse. If you click on an object with the **Information** button clicked, the box in the upper right-hand corner of the screen shows you all of the data associated with the object. If the artifact is a tool, you will see a generalized picture of that tool type, along with a definition, in the lower right-hand corner.

Choose the unit that you just excavated, and plot an X-Y map of the material recovered from one of your levels (choose a level that has quite a bit of material). Look at the distribution of artifacts within the level. Click on several of the artifacts to see more information on them.

Draw a plan map of ten of the artifacts, bones, or rocks in the unit on the graph paper on the next page. Use the X and Y coordinates provided for each artifact in the upper left-hand portion of your screen in drawing your map.

Now look at the X-Y plots of the other levels in the unit you excavated. Do you see any patterns in the distribution of artifacts and rocks?

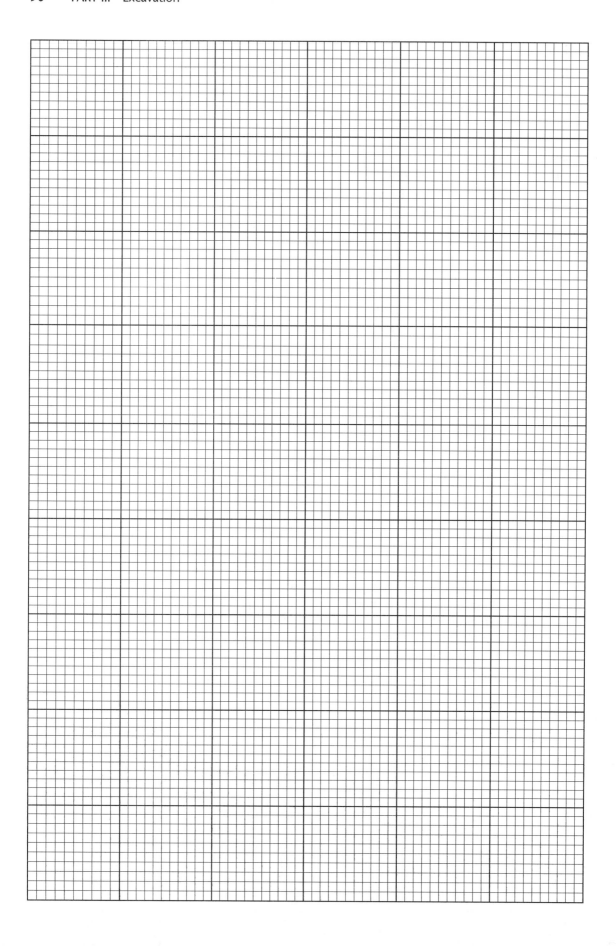

EXERCISE 13.3

Excavation of Your Virtual Project

Open your virtual project file. Design an excavation strategy based on the proposal and budget you worked on in the Setup module. Decide which units you want to dig, the methods you will use to define your stratigraphy (natural versus arbitrary levels), whether you will point provenience, what percentage of the material you will screen, and what tools you will use. Make sure that you have purchased the proper equipment for the project, and keep track of your budget!

After you have established the methods you will use, you can use either interactive excavation or automatic excavation (or both) to excavate your units. Here is a hint: Often the best plan is to excavate one square interactively and then, once the natural stratigraphy is defined, excavate contiguous units automatically by following the stratigraphy of the first unit. Be careful, however, because the stratigraphy may differ in different parts of the site.

Describe under each item below why you chose to do what you did.

Unit location:

Stratigraphy:

Proveniencing:

Screening:

Excavation tools:

So far you have generated three basic kinds of data. The first is provenience data (the X, Y, and Z coordinates of the objects), which you can view in the **Plot Excavated Artifacts** screen. From the field notebooks you can also get information on the stratigraphy of your units and counts of basic artifact classes. At this point, do you feel that you can adequately address your research questions? If not, what kind of additional data do you think you would need?

Flintknapping: The Making of Stone Tools 14

B ecause *Virtual Dig* is based on excavations conducted at a Paleolithic site, we focus on lithic (stone tool) analysis as an example of the kinds of analysis you would carry out on any excavation project. This chapter and the next three provide you with an overview of lithic technology and typology and discuss the ways you can analyze lithics. We include in these chapters a series of exercises to help familiarize you with these concepts in preparation for analyzing your virtual project assemblage.

Lithic technology refers to the way stone tools were made. Traditionally the manufacture of lithic implements involves three basic techniques: chipping or flaking, pecking, and grinding. Pecking and grinding are recent innovations, developed within the last 10,000 years, that are often used together. Pecking, which is used both for the production of implements and for certain forms of rock art, consists of pounding on the surface of a rock with a hard hammer, removing small bits of material with each blow until a desired shape is achieved. Grinding involves rubbing the stone artifact with an abrasive material. This action removes material slowly and produces a smooth surface on the artifact.

Chipped stone technology, or flintknapping, is the oldest of the three techniques and consists of many different techniques. With flintknapping, flakes are removed from pieces of raw material, such as a nodule of flint, by striking the material with a hammerstone or a piece of antler or wood (percussion technique) or by applying pressure against an edge (pressure technique). The application of either kind of force creates a conchoidal fracture that cleaves through the material until it intersects with an exterior surface, thus producing a flake. The surface of the nodule that was struck is called the striking platform and is usually preserved on the flake. After this first flake removal, the nodule is considered to be a core, and additional flakes can be removed from any or all of its surfaces. During the process of flintknapping a large amount of debitage, or debris, is produced, usually in the form of small flakes and flake fragments.

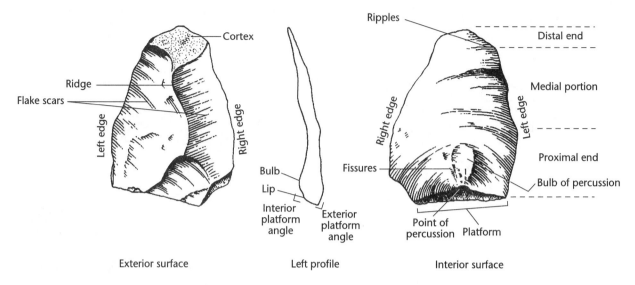

Flake landmarks

TERMINOLOGY AND FLAKE LANDMARKS

A flake can be recognized by certain characteristics. Flakes have both interior and exterior surfaces. The exterior surface is the surface that represents the original core surface, and the interior surface represents the fracture plane that separated the flake from the core. The exterior surface may have traces of cortex (the original, weathered surface of the exterior of the raw material) or flake scars from previous flake removals. The point of percussion is the exact point on the platform where the core was struck. The platform represents the proximal end of the flake, and the end opposite the platform is called the distal end. The lateral margins are the sides of the flake.

Flakes have a bulb of percussion, which is a bulge or protuberance on the interior surface of the flake just below the point of percussion. Ripples may be present below the bulb of percussion and represent the dispersal of the force. Fissures or tiny cracks may appear near the bulb; these will be more or less parallel to the axis of force and let you know the direction of the force even if the platform is missing. These characteristics are used to help distinguish man-made from natural breakage.

FLAKING TECHNIQUES

The size and shape of a flake will depend on certain characteristics of the platform, the morphology of the core surface, and the manner in which force is applied to the raw material. The most common techniques seen in the Paleolithic are described in the following list:

- *Hard-hammer percussion* involves removing a flake from a core using a hammerstone that is made of material harder than the material being flaked. Hard-hammer percussion will leave distinct marks on a flake, including a point of percussion on the flake platform, a well-developed bulb of percussion, and clear ripples.

- *Soft-hammer percussion* involves using a softer hammer of bone, wood, or antler to remove flakes. Soft-hammer percussion is used to shape tools and is especially common in the production of bifaces. These flakes have smaller, more diffuse bulbs of percussion, usually have smaller platforms, and often exhibit a distinctive lip visible on their platforms on the interior side.

- *Pressure flaking* involves using the tip of an antler to remove a series of small flakes by applying pressure to the blank edge. Pressure flaking can be done either to shape the edge of tools or to dull one side of a flake so that it can be held during tool use.

- *Blade core reduction* involves removing a series of long blades from a core. Blades are defined as flakes that are at least twice as long as they are wide. The removal of the first blade develops a ridge system for the succeeding blades to follow (Whittaker 1994:221). Blades can be removed by using direct percussion or by striking an antler punch that is set up on the platform of the core. Blade production is a more efficient means of core reduction, because you are able to produce more cutting edge per core than with flake production, and the blades are standardized.

- *Bipolar reduction* is done when very small cobbles of raw material make hard-hammer percussion difficult. With bipolar reduction the cobble is placed on another hard surface (known as an anvil) and then the top of the cobble is hit with a hammerstone. Bipolar reduction leaves distinct evidence of crushing where the core sat on the anvil.

- *Prepared core technologies* involve preparing the surfaces of cores prior to flake removal to ensure the removal of a specific shape of flake. With careful preparation of the core the flintknapper is better able to control the outcome of his or her flintknapping. The most common core preparation technique during the Middle Paleolithic is known as Levallois, which was used to obtain large, flat flakes, blades, and points.

LITHIC ANALYSIS

Lithic analysis involves looking at two major criteria: (1) lithic technology, or the way the lithics were made; and (2) lithic typology, or the different classes, or types, of artifacts within an assemblage. When doing lithic analysis you look not only at the individual pieces of stone but also at the assemblage or group of artifacts that were found together.

To introduce you to lithic analysis, in the following chapters we cover three basic concepts: lithic measurements, lithic attributes, and lithic typology. The goal is for you to learn about these concepts so that you can apply them in analyzing the lithic assemblage from your virtual project at Combe-Capelle.

Suggested Readings

Bordaz 1970; Bordes 1961b; Whittaker 1994

EXERCISE 14.1

Flintknapping Primer

You can make a flake for yourself by choosing **Flintknapping Primer** under the **Lithics Lab** menu or by clicking on the **Flintknapping Primer** option on the main screen. When you click on the **Flake Simulator** tab you will see three views of a core. You can change many of the parameters affecting flake morphology by dragging on the large red dots. To make a flake, click on the red line shown on the platform surface. Experiment with different shapes and angles to see the effect they have on the resulting flake.

With its typically sharp edges, a flake is potentially useful as a tool without further modification, but often it is further shaped and modified. Flakes that are sufficiently large or have other characteristics that make them potential tools are called blanks. Retouching, which modifies the shape of a tool, involves the removal of smaller flakes from the edge of a flake blank, usually in an attempt to shape the working edge of the tool. The finished product is called a flake tool. Tools can be retouched either unifacially (one side) or bifacially (two sides), and after they are used they can be resharpened or further retouched to transform them into another tool type. The tools recovered at an archaeological site are the final products of this reduction sequence.

The **Tool Retoucher** tab allows you to retouch a flake that you just made. First make a flake and then click the **Save for Retouching** button. You will be taken to a screen that reproduces the flake you just made. Clicking closer to the edge will remove a larger retouch flake; clicking farther away will make it smaller. Try experimenting to see what kinds of tools you can make. If you produce something that you would like to save or return to later, click on the **Save Image** button and give it a name. You can retrieve it later using the **Load Image** button and continue retouching it at that time. You can also load some examples of major tool types that are supplied on the *Virtual Dig* CD-ROM.

Just as in real flintknapping, it is easy to make a mistake. When most flintknappers make a mistake they simply rework the piece until it looks the way they want it.

After you have made a tool the way you want, you can print it or email the saved image to your instructor.

Basics of Lithic Analysis I: Lithic Measurements

M easurements are an important part of lithic analysis. Six standard measurements are taken on flakes and tools:

1. *Length* is measured from the point of percussion on the platform to the distal end of the flake.
2. *Width* can be measured as width at midpoint of length, maximum width, or both. A point in the center of the length axis is used to measure the width; measurements are taken from margin to margin and perpendicular to the length axis. Maximum width is also taken perpendicular to the length axis but at the point where the measurement would be the widest.
3. *Thickness* is measured at the midpoint of the length axis, or where the width axis crosses the length axis.
4. *Platform width* is measured from one lateral margin of the platform to the other.
5. *Platform thickness* is measured at the point of percussion from the interior to the exterior surface of the flake.
6. *Weight* is usually recorded using a gram scale.

You can use the CD-ROM to learn more about these measurements. Start *Virtual Dig*, and then choose **Lithic Measurements** from the **Lithics Lab** menu.

Measurements can be taken with calipers, and some data entry programs allow electronic calipers to be linked directly to a computer program so that measurements are entered automatically.

Consistency is an important requirement in measuring lithics. In a study of analytical consistency, Fish (1978) found that interanalyst variability in taking measurements was significant. In other words, different people don't always get the same answer when they take the same measurement. Measurements must be taken in a consistent manner, and you must explicitly define how each measurement was taken.

Flake and tool size can provide information on how raw materials were used and on the technology used to reduce cores and make tools. During the initial stages of core reduction, larger and heavier flakes are produced, whereas continued reduction results in the production of smaller flakes. If raw material is used heavily, you may find a substantial number of small flakes in an assemblage, although the initial size of the raw material cobble will also influence flake size. Bulk weights (for example, from a level) can provide information on the amount of material for comparison between levels at a site.

Tool size can provide information on the blanks chosen for making tools and on the amount of tool reduction. At many Middle Paleolithic sites, large blanks were selected for tool production. This was determined by comparing the measurements of flakes and tools. In developing his model of scraper reduction, Dibble (1995) found that scrapers were not reduced beyond a certain width and were discarded once they reached that width. That is, there was a size limit to the amount of tool reduction typically done on a piece.

Platform measurements can provide information on the original size of a blank, which is vital for assessing the amount of tool reduction (Dibble 1997). If the platform size is very large in relation to the final size of the tool, the original blank was likely much larger before it was reduced by resharpening.

Suggested Readings

Debénath and Dibble 1994; Whittaker 1994

EXERCISE 15.1

Lithic Measurements

Start *Virtual Dig,* and choose **Lithic Measurements** from the **Lithics Lab** menu. The first tab shows you how the various measurements are taken.

Click on the **Practice Measuring** tab. The image on the right-hand side is the first artifact that you will measure, shown in plan view (for measuring length, width, and maximum width), side view (for measuring thickness), and platform view (for measuring platform width and thickness). The point of percussion is indicated by the red arrow with a cross through the stem.

To take a measurement, first click on the measurement name. Then click the mouse over the spot on the artifact where you want to start taking the measurement, move the mouse to the end point of the measurement, and click again. The value of the measurement (in millimeters) is then displayed next to the measurement name. If the value is shown in black, your measurement is within acceptable limits; otherwise, it is shown in red. If you want to change a measurement, just repeat these steps.

After you are finished taking all six measurements, move the scroll bar at the bottom of the image to the next artifact and take the same six measurements. Do this for all ten artifacts.

The **Practice Results** tab summarizes the measurements you have taken on all of the artifacts. You may print this spreadsheet and turn it in to your instructor.

Basics of Lithic Analysis II: Lithic Attributes

16

I n doing lithic analysis, you can use a variety of qualitative attributes to examine lithic technology and typology. These attributes can be used to classify and compare artifacts within and among assemblages. The most common attributes used in Paleolithic lithic analysis include cortex and blank form. For tools, the number of retouched edges and retouch intensity are important attributes. Other attributes can be used to address specific research questions.

COMMON LITHIC ATTRIBUTES

You can use the CD-ROM to learn about some common lithic attributes. Start *Virtual Dig,* and then choose **Stone Tool Attributes** from the **Lithics Lab** menu. The tabs will give you examples for recording four attributes: cortex, blank form, number of retouched edges, and retouch intensity.

- *Cortex* refers to the amount of cortex (the original exterior surface of the raw material) visible on the flake. It is usually recorded as a percentage of the visible flake surface. Flakes are often classified, based on the percentage of cortex, as primary (having cortex covering virtually all of the exterior surface), secondary (with some cortex), and tertiary (with very little or no cortex). At Combe-Capelle we made an even finer distinction, noting cortex as 0%, 1–10%, 10–40%, 40–60%, 60–90%, 90–100%. Cortex is sometimes used to determine whether core reduction or tool production was practiced at a site. For example, the predominance of cortical flakes is seen as representing an emphasis on primary (initial) core reduction, whereas a preponderance of noncortical flakes is seen as evidence of tool production. There are problems inherent in this approach, however, because the amount of cortex is tied very closely to the size of the nodules of raw material. If you have large nodules of raw material, the cortex will be removed relatively quickly, leaving a large number of partially cortical and noncortical flakes. Cortex in and of itself cannot be used to infer technology, but it can be used to complement other attributes in examining technology.

- *Blank form* refers to the basic shape of a flake, which can be indicative of certain kinds of technologies (for example, blade core technology). Blank form categories will often be regionally or temporally specific. The categories of blank form used for lithic analysis at Combe-Capelle included angular, flake blade, blade, point, and normal. Angular blanks have a very high exterior ridge. A flake blade is a piece whose length is more than twice its width; blades also fit this definition but exhibit parallel flake scars on their exterior surfaces. Points are blanks whose edges converge to form a point. All others are classified as normal.

- *Number of retouched edges* is an attribute that is relevant only to tools. It refers to the number of edges (of the distal, proximal, and two lateral edges) that exhibit retouch.

- *Retouch intensity* refers to the amount of retouch present on a tool edge. At Combe-Capelle it was measured qualitatively according to four ordered categories of retouch intensity: (1) light—shallow and sometimes discontinuous retouch with little alteration of the flake edge, (2) medium—retouch that is continuous and moderately invasive (extends into the tool edge), (3) heavy—very steep or invasive, and (4) stepped—heavy retouch with tiered or stacked retouch scars. In Paleolithic studies, stepped and overlapping retouch is called Quina retouch. These categories were defined to take into account both the invasiveness of the retouch and the increase in edge angle that can result from repeated resharpening.

OTHER LITHIC ATTRIBUTES IN THE COMBE-CAPELLE DATA

The data from Combe-Capelle included other commonly used lithic attributes that you can use in your analysis of the material from your virtual project:

- *Dataclass* refers to the basic kinds of lithics in an assemblage. These include complete flakes and tools (with intact platforms, flake margins, and distal ends), proximal pieces (with intact platforms and flake margins but lacking distal ends), flake fragments (or medial/distal fragments lacking platforms), and shatter or debris. The percentage of each of these dataclasses within an assemblage may provide information on lithic technology. For example, a high percentage of complete flakes and debris is often associated with core reduction, whereas a higher percentage of flake fragments is often associated with tool production (Sullivan and Rozen 1985).

   Other dataclasses in the Combe-Capelle database include complete and fragmentary cores, bifaces, manuports (unworked material), rocks (limestone blocks), rognons (flint nodules), and unworked (thermally fractured flint or other natural rocks that were mistakenly considered to be artifacts during excavation).

- *Platform* refers to the preparation of the platform exhibited on a flake. It can indicate the type of core reduction used. The most common platform types are cortical (the platform is covered with cortex), plain (without cortex or any other preparation), dihedral (two facets, or small flakes, removed from the platform surface), and faceted (three or more facets). Plain and cortical platforms are often associated with the initial stages of core reduction, whereas faceted platforms are often associated with tool production.

- *Technology* refers to the technology used to produce flakes. The basic technologies recognized at Combe-Capelle were Levallois, blade, retouch (including biface retouch and retouch flakes), normal, and other.

- *Alteration* refers to changes in the artifacts after they were made. The most common alteration at Combe-Capelle is patina, which is a lightening of the natural color of the flint resulting from chemical action. We recorded four kinds of patina: no patina, light patina, heavy patina, and full patina. Other possible categories for alteration are burned, rolled, and other.

- *Edge damage* refers to small nicks on the edges of flakes that often result from postdepositional disturbance. We recorded four kinds of edge damage at Combe-Capelle: none, exterior (that is, on the exterior surface of the flake), interior, or both.

- *Percentage of cortex* refers to a numeric value we computed based on the midpoint of the cortex category range. In other words, flakes with a cortex category of 40–60% were given a value of 50 for percentage of cortex. This enabled us to treat cortex as both numeric and character variables.

- *Raw material* refers to the kinds of lithic raw materials that were being used at Combe-Capelle. Most of the flint is local, but a small percentage is exotic to the site and must have been transported in.

For various reasons, all of the possible attributes will not be visible on every lithic artifact, and some attributes are not relevant to particular kinds of objects. When these cases occurred at Combe-Capelle, the attribute in question was given a value of "Missing." Such values are automatically excluded from your analysis of your virtual project.

ANALYZING LITHIC ATTRIBUTES

At Combe-Capelle, lithic attributes were useful for examining how raw materials were used. One of our primary research questions concerned how raw materials were used at the site. The site is located on a raw material source, and we expected that the availability of raw materials may have been one of the main reasons that Middle Paleolithic groups went to Combe-Capelle. This hypothesis was confirmed by our analysis. For example, because the lower levels of Sector I showed evidence of the early stages of core reduction, it appears that raw materials were quarried in these levels. These levels have more complete flakes and more cortical flakes than the other levels at the site, and the platforms were primarily plain or cortical. We found that a very high percentage of the lithics at the site were made of local flint, and tools were made of nonlocal material more often than were flakes, indicating that the tools were imported. We also found low retouch intensity and a low average number of retouched edges, indicating that the tools were not heavily reduced. This was consistent with the abundance of raw material at the site.

EXERCISE 16.1

Lithic Attributes

Under the **Lithics Lab** menu, choose **Stone Tool Attributes** and click on the **Cortex** tab. Choose the appropriate value for this attribute from the list provided in the lower right-hand portion of the screen under the artifact, and then use the scroll bar to select the next artifact. Repeat these steps for each of the attribute tabs. When you are finished, click on the **Practice Results** tab to see your tabulated answers. Correct answers are shown in black, and incorrect answers are shown in red. You may go back and change values at any time. When you are satisfied with your results you may print the spreadsheet from the **Practice Results** page.

Basics of Lithic Analysis III: Lithic Typology

17

Typology is one of the most important analytical tools for the archaeologist. It is a way to organize and classify artifacts to facilitate analysis. Types are defined as a set (or cluster) of attributes shared by a group, making them more similar to one another than to other groups. The attributes most commonly used to define types include form, technology, function, style, and the amount of reduction. Types can thus be defined based on the attributes that you are most interested in and that will help you answer your research questions. For example, you may choose to focus on certain attributes such as flake form and edge angle to look at tool function, whereas another researcher may focus on flake form, cortex, and size to look at raw material use. There are thus no "ideal" types in the sense that an artifact is or is not a certain type; it depends on the attributes you examine.

Typologies are most useful as a way of organizing and comparing data. They are most often constructed for pottery and lithic tools. For example, each region of the United States has a standard projectile point typology that is used to classify projectile points found within that region. Although you may use a general type to classify your projectile points, you can also focus on other aspects of the points outside that classification, which would necessitate the construction of your own typology for analysis.

Several types can co-occur on a regular basis; these form an assemblage, or group of types that are consistently found together, and usually reflect shared activities. Assemblages can provide information on site function, and changes in artifact assemblages over time have been an important means for examining past cultural change.

THE TYPOLOGY OF FRANÇOIS BORDES

As we discussed in Chapter 2, the explanation of typological variability has been a major focus of Middle Paleolithic research. The standard typology used by Paleolithic researchers was developed by François Bordes (1961b). Bordes defined 63 different tool types for the Lower and Middle Paleolithic, and these types form the basis of lithic analysis in Paleolithic research today. They were defined on the basis of several criteria—technology (especially

109

Levallois or not), the type of retouch, its location on particular edges, and the shape of the edge. Most of the types are retouched, but some are not.

Because lithics were the primary artifact class recovered at Combe-Capelle, it is important that you understand at least the basics of Bordes's typology.

Four classes of tools either occur with some frequency in Paleolithic assemblages or are important for the classification of different Middle Paleolithic assemblage groups. These are scrapers, notches and denticulates, technologically defined tools, and bifaces.

Scrapers

Scrapers are the most frequently occurring tool in the European Middle Paleolithic, and they are the major typological group in both the Quina and Ferrassie Mousterian. More subdivisions exist among the scrapers than among any other typological group in Bordes's typology.

A scraper is a flake tool with continuous retouch on one or more edges. Bordes emphasized the functional aspect of these tools, and he thought that scraper retouch was not meant to sharpen the edge of a tool but rather to regularize it and even to partially blunt it in order to give it more resistance for scraping. However, it is by no means certain that all scrapers were used for scraping; they could easily have been used as cutting tools or for other tasks. Like most stone tools in the Lower and Middle Paleolithic, they were probably used for a variety of tasks. For this reason, the use of the term *scraper* is probably not fully justified, but it is a name with which almost all archaeologists are familiar. It is also likely that most of the major scraper types defined by Bordes are more or less arbitrary partitions along a continuum of reduction of blanks through resharpening. Although this fact does not affect the typology of these tools, it does have implications for the interpretation of these various types.

In Bordes's typology, the major classes of scrapers are defined on the basis of the number of, the location of, and the relation between the retouched edges. Within most of the major scraper classes, minor subdivisions are made at the level of the individual type for differences in edge shape (that is, straight, convex, or concave), as seen from the exterior surface of the flake. If the edge has a combination of edge shapes, such as straight and convex, then it is classified according to the longest or most pronounced portion.

Scrapers are divided into four subclasses: (1) single scrapers with retouch along one lateral edge (with three defined types differentiated on the basis of edge shape); (2) double scrapers, with two lateral retouched edges (with six different types based on edge shape); (3) convergent scrapers, with two lateral retouched edges that meet at the distal end (four types including déjeté scrapers, plus Mousterian points and limaces); and (4) transverse scrapers, which have scraper retouch on a broad edge located on the distal end (including three types). There are other, rarer scraper types, including scrapers with thinned backs; alternate, abrupt, and bifacial scrapers; and scrapers on the interior surface.

Notches and Denticulates

The second major class of tools comprises the notches and denticulates, which represent the other most commonly occurring types in the Middle Paleolithic. They are the principal types represented in Denticulate Mousterian assemblages.

However, they have few common characteristics as a group. They can occur on virtually any kind of blank, they can take any shape, and the retouch can be on the interior as well as the exterior. In spite of this variability, Bordes's typology makes relatively few typological distinctions within this class, which is somewhat surprising given the number of scraper types.

A notch is a relatively deep concavity on a flake edge. Notches can be made with a single blow or by a series of small contiguous removals that hollow out a concavity. The dimensions of the concavity (that is, the depth and width) are quite variable. Three types of notches are distinguished by Bordes: notches, end-notched pieces, and notched triangles.

Denticulates, or "tooth-edged" pieces, are flakes with two or more contiguous notches. The intersection of these notches forms a series of points or spines, although these can be fairly rounded. One denticulate subtype is the Tayac Point, which has two converging denticulate edges.

Technologically Defined Types

The third major class in Bordes's typology includes the technologically defined types. These types are defined on the basis of the technology used to produce them (and therefore their shape) rather than on a particular kind of retouch.

Levallois flakes and points are important elements for characterizing Middle Paleolithic industries. As mentioned earlier, Levallois technology is defined as a way of preparing a core surface in order to get a particular shape of flake. Bordes recognized two kinds of Levallois flakes in his typology, typical and atypical. He also had types for Levallois points and pseudo-Levallois points, the latter of which is not really Levallois at all but is the result of what is called disc-core technology.

Another important type is the naturally backed knife, which is an unretouched flake or blade that has a sharp cutting edge on one margin and a natural cortical surface (the "back") on the opposing edge. The cortical surface is perpendicular, or nearly so, to the interior surface. This is different from another type, the backed knife, where the backing is deliberately put on the piece with abrupt retouch. These pieces are similar to modern pocket knives that have a blade with one sharp edge opposite a blunted edge.

With all of these technologically defined tools the presence of retouch overrides the technological category. For example, if a Levallois flake is retouched into a scraper, then it is typed as a scraper and the Levallois technology is noted elsewhere. The same is true for a naturally backed knife with a notch on one of its edges; it would be classified as a notch and not a naturally backed knife. However, unlike flakes made with other, nondiagnostic technologies, the presence of edge damage on any of these technologically defined types does not result in its classification in the type of abrupt and alternating retouch.

Bifaces

The fourth major class of tools in Bordes's typology is bifaces. Bifaces, or handaxes, are bifacially flaked tools. This category includes a range of tool types that are distinguished primarily on the basis of their thickness and shape. Bifaces are very common in Acheulian (Lower Paleolithic) industries but less common in the Middle Paleolithic. Their presence defines one major Mousterian assemblage type, the Mousterian of Acheulian Tradition (MTA).

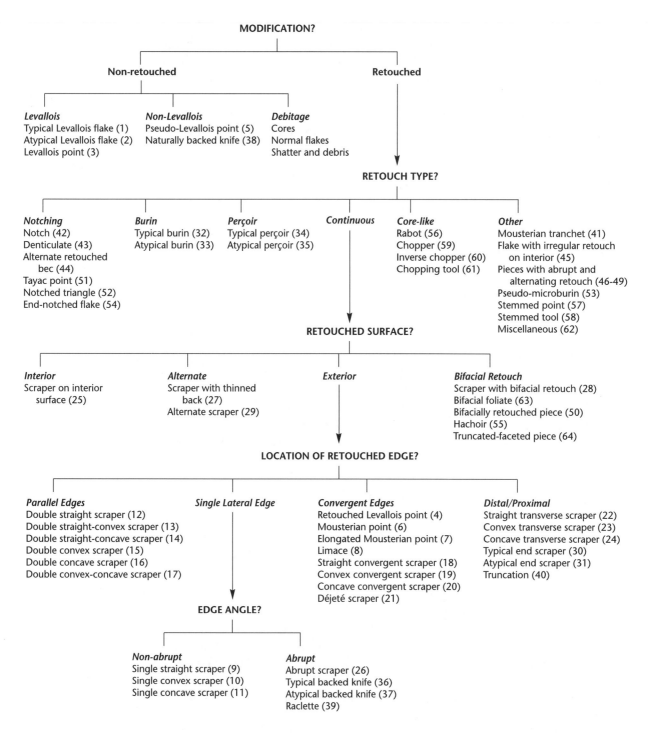

Flowchart for determining stone tool types, with Bordes's type number given in parenthesis.
(Data from Debénath and Dibble, 1994)

Because no two lithic artifacts are alike, learning lithic typology requires many years of experience. One way to approach it is to break down the classification process into a series of questions in a hierarchical format as a kind of flowchart. By answering the questions, you can follow a path that helps you narrow down the choices of appropriate types. This is how we have organized the type list in the **Lithic Typology** option of the **Lithics Lab** menu.

BORDIAN GRAPHS AND INDICES

Bordes used the percentages of these tool types to compare Mousterian assemblages from different geological levels within a site and between sites. First, he assigned a number for each of his types (1–63), which allowed him to present the counts for each type in a specific order (Table 17.1). Next, he calculated the relative percentages of each type by dividing the number of one type by the total number of tools in the assemblage. For example, if there are 10 single straight scrapers (type 9) in an assemblage of 125 tools, then the percentage of type 9 would be 10/125, or 8 percent. He then computed the cumulative percentage following the numbered order of the type list. To compute the cumulative percentage you start with the percentage of type 1. You then add the percentage of type 2 to this, then add the percentage of type 3, and so on. At the end you will reach 100 percent. You can see an example of this on the **Type Lists** tab on the **Lithic Typology** screen.

Bordes displayed the distribution of types in an assemblage using a cumulative graph, which has the ordered type numbers on the horizontal (X) axis and the cumulative percentage as one proceeds along the type list on the vertical (Y) axis. Where the line goes up steeply, a relatively high percentage of that type is present in an assemblage. Cumulative graphs allow you to see the contribution of the percentage of each tool type relative to the others for an assemblage and to compare the typological makeup of different assemblages. You can see an example of this on the **Cumulative Graphs** tab on the **Lithic Typology** screen.

In addition to his type list and cumulative graphs, Bordes developed a number of indices that can be used to describe Mousterian assemblages. These indices are broken down into typological indices, which are based on the type list, and technological indices, which are based on other lithic attributes. The principal typological indices are as follows:

- *Levallois typological index* (ILty) measures the percentage of Levallois types (types 1–4) in the tool assemblage (the total of types 1–4 divided by the total of types 1–63).
- *Scraper index* (IR) measures the percentage of scrapers (types 9–29) in the tool assemblage.
- *Notching index* (NI) measures the percentage of notched tools (types 42–44, 51, 52, 54) in the tool assemblage.

When Bordes was first studying Mousterian assemblages, he recognized that one of the keys to documenting variability in these assemblages was technology. He was especially interested in the difference between Levallois and bifacial core-reduction techniques. As a result, he developed several technological indices for comparing assemblages using the attributes discussed earlier in this chapter:

- *Levallois index* (IL) looks at the percentage of all items made using the Levallois technique in an assemblage (all retouched and unretouched pieces). If the percentage is above 25 percent, the assemblage is considered to be

Table 17.1   The Type List of François Bordes

Type Number	Type Name	Major Class
1	Typical Levallois flake	Levallois
2	Atypical Levallois flake	Levallois
3	Levallois point	Levallois
4	Retouched Levallois point	Levallois
5	Pseudo-Levallois point	Technological type
6	Mousterian point	Point
7	Elongated Mousterian point	Point
8	Limace	Scraper
9	Single straight scraper	Scraper
10	Single convex scraper	Scraper
11	Single concave scraper	Scraper
12	Double straight scraper	Scraper
13	Double straight-convex scraper	Scraper
14	Double straight-concave scraper	Scraper
15	Double convex scraper	Scraper
16	Double concave scraper	Scraper
17	Double concave-convex scraper	Scraper
18	Single convergent scraper	Scraper
19	Convex convergent scraper	Scraper
20	Concave convergent scraper	Scraper
21	Déjeté scraper	Scraper
22	Straight transverse scraper	Scraper
23	Convex transverse scraper	Scraper
24	Concave transverse scraper	Scraper
25	Scraper on interior surface	Scraper
26	Abrupt scraper	Scraper
27	Scraper with thinned back	Scraper
28	Scraper with bifacial retouch	Scraper
29	Alternate scraper	Scraper
30	Typical endscraper	Upper Paleolithic type
31	Atypical endscraper	Upper Paleolithic type
32	Typical burin	Upper Paleolithic type
33	Atypical burin	Upper Paleolithic type
34	Typical perçoir	Upper Paleolithic type
35	Atypical perçoir	Upper Paleolithic type
36	Typical backed knife	Upper Paleolithic type
37	Atypical backed knife	Upper Paleolithic type
38	Naturally backed knife	Technological type
39	Raclette	Upper Paleolithic type
40	Truncation	Upper Paleolithic type
41	Mousterian tranchet	Miscellaneous
42	Notch	Notch/Denticulate
43	Denticulate	Notch/Denticulate

Table 17.1 *(continued)*

Type Number	Type Name	Major Class
44	Alternate retouched bec	Notch/Denticulate
45	Flake with irregular retouch on interior	Damage
46–49	Flake with abrupt and alternating retouch	Damage
50	Bifacially retouched flake	Miscellaneous
51	Tayac point	Notch/Denticulate
52	Notched triangle	Notch/Denticulate
53	Pseudo-microburin	Miscellaneous
54	End-notched flake	Notch/Denticulate
55	Hachoir	Miscellaneous
56	Rabot	Miscellaneous
57	Stemmed point	Point
58	Stemmed tool	Miscellaneous
59	Chopper	Miscellaneous
60	Inverse chopper	Miscellaneous
61	Chopping tool	Miscellaneous
62	Miscellaneous	Miscellaneous
63	Bifacial foliate	Point
64	Truncated-faceted piece	Miscellaneous

Levallois. You can calculate this index by selecting the **Statistics, Tables, and Graphs** option and using the Technique field.

- *Faceting index* (IF) looks at the percentage of faceted platforms (often associated with Levallois technology) in an assemblage. If an assemblage has more than 45 percent faceted platforms, it is considered to have a high faceting index. You can calculate this index by selecting the **Statistics, Tables, and Graphs** option and using the Platform field.

- *Blade index* (Ilam) records the percentage of blades in an assemblage and is used to help determine whether an assemblage has characteristics of an Upper Paleolithic assemblage. You can calculate this index by selecting the **Statistics, Tables, and Graphs** option and using the Blank Form field (and combining both "blades" and "flake blades").

- *Quina index* (IQ) refers to the number of scraper tools (types 8–29) that exhibit Quina (or stepped) retouch relative to the total number of scrapers. You can calculate this index by selecting the **Statistics, Tables, and Graphs** option and using the Retouch Intensity field.

TYPOLOGY AT COMBE-CAPELLE

At Combe-Capelle we classified all tools using Bordes's typology, with only two differences. First, we collapsed types 46–49 into one type, called type 48. Second, we added a type to Bordes's list, type 64, for truncated-faceted pieces. We also calculated the technological and typological indices used by Bordes to examine and compare the assemblages.

EXERCISE 17.1

Learning Bordian Typology

Start *Virtual Dig* and choose the **Lithic Typology** option from the **Lithics Lab** menu. The opening tab is labeled **Learn the Types**.

On the box in the upper left-hand portion of the opening screen are the questions shown in the flowchart in this chapter. When you click on the appropriate answer, the program takes you to the next level of questions until you arrive at the choice of types. When you click on one of these types, you will see a definition of the type in the box just below the type list.

A series of ten idealized artifact drawings is viewable in the box in the upper right-hand corner of the **Learn the Types** screen. You can browse through them by clicking on the scroll bar at the bottom. For each artifact, answer the questions on the left until you arrive at the correct type. You will know when you are correct because the image of the type shown on the bottom will match the image of the artifact drawing on top.

Now click on the **Type Real Artifacts** tab. Here the practice pieces are images of real artifacts from Combe-Capelle, and you can try to find the correct type using the methods you used on the **Learn the Types** screen. To see your answers, click on the **Practice Results** tab. Print the results so that you can turn them in to your instructor.

EXERCISE 17.2

Learning Bordian Type Lists and Cumulative Graphs

To learn how Bordian type lists and cumulative graphs work, click on the **Type Lists** tab of the **Lithic Typology** screen. Here you will see the type counts of a hypothetical Middle Paleolithic assemblage characteristic of a Typical Mousterian, along with the relative and cumulative percentages. Click on the **Cumulative Graphs** tab to see the shape of the graph.

You can change the composition of this assemblage by changing the count of any type on the **Type Lists** tab (be sure to press **Enter** after typing in the new number), and then see what effect your changes have on the shape of the cumulative graph. Make the following kinds of changes and print the cumulative graph for each:

1. Try adjusting the type counts so that you have an assemblage rich in single, double, and convergent scrapers and Mousterian points and a relatively high number of Levallois flakes and points. This kind of assemblage is characteristic of a Ferrassie Mousterian.

2. Now adjust the type counts so that you have very few Levallois flakes and points, fewer double and convergent scrapers, but relatively more transverse scrapers. This kind of assemblage is characteristic of a Quina Mousterian.

3. Now, to see an example of what a Denticulate Mousterian looks like, lower the number of scrapers in general, but increase the number of notches and denticulates.

EXERCISE 17.3

Making Scrapers

Go to the **Flintknapping Primer** under the **Lithics Lab** menu. First make a flake, save it for retouching, and then retouch it to make the following types in this order:

1. Notch
2. Denticulate
3. Single convex scraper
4. Double straight scraper
5. Convex convergent scraper
6. Convex transverse scraper

Is there a point in this process when you have to make a new flake and start over? In other words, for example, can a denticulate be transformed into a single convex scraper? Can a convergent scraper be transformed into a transverse one?

What does this tell you about the processes through which stone tools can be re-modified and reshaped as they are used?

Overview of
Archaeological Analysis

18

During excavation, you collect a large number of artifacts and other material. The next stage in a field project involves analyzing that material so that you can begin to answer your research questions and understand what was going on at the site when it was occupied. In this chapter and the next two, we discuss the basics of data analysis.

Assessing site taphonomy, or the processes involved in site formation, is also an important part of any field project, but it is especially important in Paleolithic studies because of the length of time the sites have been buried and because they may have been disturbed by a variety of geological processes. Chapter 20 includes an exercise on evaluating site taphonomy that can be applied to your virtual project.

DAY-TO-DAY PRACTICES IN A LAB

The lab is where you process and analyze the artifacts after they are recovered during excavation. Typically, either the material is brought directly to the lab from the excavation site or preliminary lab work (for example, washing and labeling) is done at a field lab. In either case, check the artifact bags to make sure that all the provenience information is recorded on them and then check the data against the field records to make sure that the information is correct. If a computerized data recording system is used, the computer analyst cleans the computerized database and then informs the lab of any changes that need to be made to the artifact bags.

After you check the material, wash, label, and sort it. Washing makes the attributes of the artifacts more visible for analysis, and labeling records provenience information. Your decision on what to wash and label depends on the number of artifacts recovered and occasionally on the requirements of the facility where you will store (curate) the artifacts after the project is completed.

Artifacts are usually washed in water, either by rubbing them with your fingers or by gently scrubbing them with a toothbrush or soft-bristled scrub brush. If you are planning to do microscopic analysis on the lithics, you should never use a scrub brush because doing so could damage the traces

Analyzing lithics in
the lab at La Forge

left on the edges. You can wash artifacts covered with heavy caliche or breccia (calcium carbonate) or other hard-to-remove material in a diluted acid bath. Keep the bag or a tag with the artifacts as they dry to ensure that their provenience information is kept. You may choose not to wash some artifacts because they will be used for specialized analysis such as residue analysis or pollen washes or simply because they are too fragile.

Once the artifacts are dry, label them using indelible ink and a quill-tipped pen or a very fine-tipped permanent marker. The label usually consists of the site name or number and some kind of catalogue number. The catalogue number will most often be the number used to designate the artifact in the field (in the case of Combe-Capelle, the unit–ID number). Often you will fill out a catalogue form to show that the artifacts have been washed and labeled. Because the catalogue number provides the link between the artifact and the data associated with it, the label must be legible. Place the label on a portion of the artifact that will not be needed for analysis; for example, do not label the edge of stone tools. After you write the label on the artifact, cover it with a layer of clear nail polish to preserve it. It is usually not necessary to label every artifact, especially if bulk artifacts are collected from a level, but you should label a sufficiently large sample so that provenience information is not lost if the artifacts are separated from their bag label or tag.

After you wash and label the artifacts, make preliminary sorts of the material. Sorting categories will depend on the type of analysis you will be doing and the way the material was collected. If you have collected bulk material by level, you may sort it into basic categories such as lithics, ceramics, and bone. If you have collected primarily one artifact type or did preliminary sorts in the field, you may sort artifacts into more specific categories. For example, lithics can be sorted into flakes, debris, and tools.

Use polyurethane bags to store the artifacts. Label the bags and include with the artifacts a tag with the provenience information. The artifacts are then ready to be given or sent to the analysts. Check all other samples (for example, pollen, dating, fauna) to make sure that they are properly bagged and that the provenience information is legible. They can then be sent to specialists for analysis or stored in boxes for future use.

Specialized analysts or trained crew members under the supervision of a specialist will carry out artifact analysis. Each analyst will record a set of attributes (observations or measurements) for the artifacts depending on the research questions they are addressing. Data from the analysts can be either written on paper and entered into a computer later or entered directly into a computerized database. The computerized data can be used for further statistical analysis or summarized in the final report.

After all of the material has been analyzed, you can prepare it for final storage or curation. Each curation facility will have specific requirements for permanent storage. In general, material should be bagged by unit, level, or both and stored in boxes. All field documents should be curated with the artifacts.

ANALYSIS AT COMBE-CAPELLE

At Combe-Capelle we processed and analyzed all of the artifacts at our laboratory at La Forge. We brought artifacts to the lab from the site at the end of each day and processed them the next day. We washed and labeled all artifacts that were mapped with the theodolite (those that were 3 cm or larger). Each artifact was labeled with "CC" (for Combe-Capelle) and the unit–ID number assigned to it in the field (for example, L1015-42). The artifact number was linked directly to the computer database so that provenience information could be retrieved easily.

We found during the initial phases of our analysis that the ID numbers written on the artifacts were often either mislabeled or illegible. This led us to develop a system that eliminated both of these problems. After the artifacts were labeled and before they were separated from their provenience tag, a person other than the one who had done the labeling read the artifact's number aloud while the first person checked it against the tag. If the person reading the number had any problems, the number was rewritten. This ensured that the label was both correct and legible to someone other than the person doing the labeling.

We brought buckets of sediments to La Forge at noon and at the end of the day (although more bucket runs were necessary if the crew was excavating quickly). We wet screened the sediment for small finds, which we bagged by the mesh size of the screen (coarse = 1 cm; fine = 2.5 mm) along with a tag containing provenience information from the EDM placed in a small plastic bag inside the larger artifact bag. The artifacts found in the screen were not labeled because of their small size, but the tag was kept with the material. If we recovered any artifact larger than 3 cm during wet screening, we separated it from the screened material, gave it the provenience information of the bucket from which it was taken, labeled it, and included it in the analysis of the larger artifacts.

The lab director and the two PI/PDs carried out the lithic analysis in the lab. They used laptop computers and entered all attribute data directly into a computerized database. They took lithic measurements with electronic calipers connected directly to the computers, eliminating data entry error. Although faunal preservation was poor, we sent the fauna that was recovered to a French faunal analyst in Bordeaux. We also sent dating and pollen samples to specialists for analysis at the end of each field season.

We stored digital images of about 10 percent of the excavated material in the computerized database. These images, many of which are included in *Virtual Dig,* provide examples of what the artifacts recovered at Combe-Capelle look like. Each image includes the original unit—ID catalogue number of the artifact and a computer-generated scale.

After we completed the analysis, we bagged all labeled artifacts in polyurethane bags by geological level and by tool type. The bags of small finds were placed together in boxes by geological level. The material is now curated at the Musée National de Préhistoire in Les Eyzies, France.

Analyzing Lithic Data with *Virtual Dig*

19

Y ou can analyze the data from Combe-Capelle using either the entire data set that came from our excavations or the data generated from your own virtual project. For the analysis of most fields, open the **Statistics, Tables, and Graphs** screen from the **Analysis** menu. The Type field is best handled under the **Creating Type Lists** screen. Because you must have data to work with in order to use this screen, you should either load Combe-Capelle data or excavate some of your own site and load your virtual project.

STATISTICS, TABLES, AND GRAPHS

Click on the **Analyze Field** tab. Many options are available on this screen; therefore, you can easily get the results you need.

First, decide what kind of artifacts you want to analyze. The choices are complete flakes, complete tools, or complete cores. By choosing one of these options, you are limiting the results to that particular group of artifacts.

You will then be given a list of variables or fields available for analysis. Each variable will be either a numeric or a character variable, which will determine the kinds of analyses you can do. Select one variable by clicking on it.

Lithic measurements are numeric data when entered into a database, and one of the most common ways to compare these measurements is to compute and compare means (averages). It is also useful to look at the standard deviation of your sample, which tells you how much variation is present within an assemblage and can be used to compare two or more assemblages to see which is more variable. Another important measure is the range, which consists of the maximum and minimum values of a particular measurement. The range is useful for examining variability within an assemblage; a low range suggests that the measurements are similar and the assemblage is homogeneous.

Sizes can also be compared by converting them into ratios. For example, the length:width ratio can be used to determine the degree of flake elongation; this can provide information on whether blade core reduction was practiced. Comparisons of the ratio of the platform to flake sizes can illustrate the amount of tool reduction in an assemblage.

Numeric variables can be compared by putting them in a data table or graph. Tables are ideal for presenting large amounts of numeric data in a compact, readable form. For example, if you are discussing artifact size, you can tailor your data table to show the mean values for flake and tool length, width, and thickness from each level you excavated.

Graphs can provide a visual representation of your data. They can supplement data tables and are used to illustrate the points you are trying to make. The most common graphs used to illustrate lithic measurements are plot (or line), HiLo, candle, and bar graphs. These graphs present the values of a particular variable for each unit or level. Differences in color or shading can be used to compare these variables from different levels at a site or from different sites.

Lithic attributes are entered into the database as character variables because they are not strictly quantified. Statistics such as the mean and standard deviation are not normally used with character variables, but counts (total number) can be made and these counts can then be used to calculate percentages or ratios that can be used to compare assemblages. Bar graphs or pie charts are often useful for illustrating these lithic attributes graphically.

You can also choose which artifacts to analyze in terms of their spatial provenience (units) or stratigraphic provenience (levels). If you choose the **For selected level(s)** option, you can select one or more levels from the list. Choose multiple levels (which will be analyzed as a group) either by pressing **Ctrl** while clicking on the level names or by dragging the mouse over the list. You can choose multiple units in the same manner. If you want to break down your results by either levels or units, then choose the **By Level** or **By Unit** option. You can still choose which levels or units to include in your analysis, but this time each level or unit will be analyzed separately. This enables you to compare different units or levels.

After you have chosen the artifacts, variable, and units and levels that you want to analyze, click on the **Calculate Statistics** button to perform the analysis. You can see the results in the box on the lower left-hand portion of the screen.

If you click on the **Add Results to Graph** button, then the current results will be added to any previous calculations you have made. You can keep adding results to the graph (or table) as long as you are using the same kind of variable (numeric or character). You can examine your combined results in tabular form (click on the **Table of Results** tab) or in graphic form (click on the **Graphs** tab), and you may print either of these by using the **File/Print Graph/Image/Spreadsheet** option. You can clear previously saved analyses by clicking on the **Clear the Graph** button on any of the tabs (**Analyze Field, Table of Results,** or **Graphs**).

The results you get will depend on the kind of variables you use. Numeric variables produce means, standard deviations, minima, maxima, and counts (N), which can be seen by clicking on the **Table of Results** and **Graphs** tabs. Certain graphs work well with numeric data. To plot the means of your data, choose the plot or bar graph options. The HiLo graph is useful for viewing the range (minimum and maximum). Candle graphs combine both range (the narrow line) and standard deviation (the thick line).

For character variables, the **Table of Results** screen shows both the counts and percentages of the different values. You can produce graphs based on either counts or percentages by clicking the appropriate option button. Bar graphs, stacking bar graphs, and pie charts work best for character variables.

ANALYZING TYPE COUNTS AND TYPOLOGICAL INDICES

The typological data is best analyzed with the **Creating Type Lists** screen, an option under the **Analysis** menu. This screen is designed to work with the Type field in your current database (either material you excavated with your virtual project or the real Combe-Capelle data) and will automatically create type lists, cumulative graphs, and the three main typological indices.

The first tab, **Make Type List,** allows you to choose the context of the artifacts being analyzed in terms of their spatial provenience (units) or stratigraphic provenience (levels). If you choose the **Pick from Levels o**ption, you can select one or more levels from the list. Choose multiple levels (which will be analyzed as a group) either by pressing **Ctrl** while clicking on the level names or by dragging the mouse over the list. You can choose multiple units in the same manner. After you have chosen the units or levels that you want to analyze, click on the **Make Type List** button to perform the analysis.

You can view the results of your analysis in four different ways. The first way is with the large box to the right of the **Make Type List** tab. After the analysis is performed, this box breaks down your results in a hierarchical fashion, beginning with tool typology (for counts broken down by major typological classes) or typological indices. Click on the small boxes with plus signs in them to see further breakdowns. Click on the **Type Spreadsheet** tab to see the type counts presented in a spreadsheet view in the order of the Bordian typology, with the values of the typological indices shown at the bottom. Click on the **Cumulative Graph** tab to see the type list in the form of a cumulative graph, and on the **Indices** tab to see a bar graph of the typological indices. You can print the results from these three pages.

The final tab, **Mousterian Facies,** allows you to compare your results with assemblages characteristic of the various Mousterian facies. Select one of the assemblages listed and then click on the **Add to Spreadsheet and Graphs** button. Now you can go back to the **Type Spreadsheet** and **Cumulative Graph** tabs and compare your results with other assemblages.

EXERCISE 19.1
Character Variables

Load the real Combe-Capelle data and choose the **Analysis/Statistics, Tables, and Graphs** option. From the **Analyze Field** tab, choose **Complete Flakes** and **Character** field type. Then click the **Alteration** field. On the right-hand side of the screen, select the **By Level** option and highlight all of the levels from Sector I. Then click on the **Calculate Statistics** button and the **Add Results to Graph** button. From the **Graphs** tab, choose the **Stacking Bar** graph type and the **Percentages** option. Do you see any change through time in terms of the amount of patina on the flakes?

EXERCISE 19.2
Numeric Variables

Load the real Combe-Capelle data and choose the **Analysis/Statistics, Tables, and Graphs** option. From the **Analyze Field** tab, choose **Complete Flakes** and **Numeric** field type. Then click the **Length** field. On the right-hand side of the screen, select the **By Level** option and highlight all of the levels from Sector I. Then click on the **Calculate Statistics** button and the **Add Results to Graph** button. From the **Graphs** tab, choose the **HiLo** graph type. Repeat these steps for the complete tools and the complete cores, adding the results to the graph each time.

1. Do you see any change through time in terms of the sizes of these artifact classes?

2. Do the lengths of tools and flakes seem to relate to each other, that is, if flakes are bigger in one level, are the tools bigger as well?

3. In general, it seems that cores are larger than both flakes and tools. Why is this so? Also, what does it mean that in general the tools are larger than the flakes?

4. Try the same thing using other fields that reflect size (for example, width, thickness, weight). Do you see the same patterns? Which field seems to show the clearest trends?

EXERCISE 19.3

Virtual Project

Load your virtual project and choose **Analysis/Creating Type Lists**.

1. For each level that you excavated, create a type list and answer the following questions:

   What is the best-represented tool class in your assemblage?

   Do you have more simple or complex scrapers?

   Does your assemblage change through time (stratigraphically)?

2. Create a type list for all levels at the site and create a cumulative graph for them. Compare the type list and cumulative graph from your virtual project with other kinds of Mousterian assemblage types.

3. Calculate the typological indices for your site.

   Levallois typological index:

   Scraper index:

   Notch index:

Based on these results, what kind of Mousterian group do you have?

Evaluating Taphonomy and Site Formation

20

Taphonomy is the study of the formation of archaeological sites. The goal of archaeology is to use physical remains recovered during excavation to interpret past behavior; however, many natural and cultural processes operate on a site after remains are deposited, altering their position and their form (Schiffer 1983, 1987). Taphonomic processes are fundamental to the interpretation of an archaeological site because they affect the integrity of the site and determine whether it is disturbed. Virtually all Paleolithic sites have experienced some degree of disturbance resulting from geological processes or cultural activities. Paleolithic archaeologists are thus concerned with the intensity of the disturbance processes and the interaction of natural and cultural processes that influence the integrity of a site.

Schick (1986) has proposed that it is more accurate to look at disturbance as a continuum that can be expressed in varying degrees when evaluating taphonomy at Paleolithic sites. Variations in the nature of these disturbance processes also exist and have different effects on archaeological materials. Some processes will move artifacts long distances and cause extensive artifact damage, whereas others may disturb the artifacts only slightly. Disturbance processes will also affect different classes of materials in different ways. For example, carnivore activity may significantly change the distribution of bones on a site, but it won't significantly affect the distribution of stone tools.

There are a variety of ways to examine taphonomic processes in the archaeological record. We focus on geological processes because they were the major taphonomic processes at Combe-Capelle. To examine these processes, we studied the geological deposits at the site (using soils and sediment analysis), artifact condition, and the density and distribution of artifacts. In *Virtual Dig,* we focus on the lithic artifacts themselves and what they can tell us about site taphonomy.

DAMAGE

Damage to the edges of artifacts can be indicative of geological disturbance, although not all geological processes that displace artifacts result in damage

Section of the site at Cagny-la-Garenne showing significant disturbance in the lower levels

to the pieces. For example, aeolian deflation, which occurs when lighter sedimentary particles are removed by wind action, leaving the once vertically stratified heavier artifacts and other material on a common surface, results in minimal lithic damage, but its effect on stratigraphic context can be disastrous. Many other processes such as mass wasting (where the sediments move as a unit) or water action (from streams or slopewash) leave obvious traces of damage on lithic artifacts, ranging from small nicks along the sharp edges to a high degree of artifact breakage. The extent to which such damage is present can help you determine the amount and kinds of disturbance to the site.

In any high-energy environment, lithic artifacts will be subjected to a high degree of stress, and stones may come into contact with one another. This will lead to a certain amount of damage to the pieces. Because the edges of stone tools are often thin and sharp, damage will be especially apparent there. This can make it difficult to distinguish natural damage from intentional retouch, although damage tends to be much more abrupt and irregular. Under conditions of sediment folding, or convolution, damage will likely occur on both sides of an artifact and significant artifact breakage may occur.

If the water flow is strong enough to transport lithic material, which can happen in stream deposits or as water runs downhill, then significant damage can occur. Most damage due to water action is quite abrupt and often causes damage to both sides of the artifact owing to the rolling or tumbling of the piece along the streambed or down the slope. This can result in significant abrasion, especially along the edges and the ridges between flake scars, and heavily rolled lithic artifacts can exhibit extremely round and smooth edges.

Assessing damage to a lithic assemblage can be done in a number of ways. One of the most simple and direct means is through macroscopic examination of the edges followed by coding for both degree and kind of damage. We did this at Combe-Capelle by noting whether the piece was damaged and, if so, whether it was damaged on the interior surface, exterior surface, or both. A second way is to calculate the amount of breakage by recording whether each flake or flake tool is complete, broken (that is, at the proximal end), or a fragment. The ratio of broken to complete pieces, or the percentage of broken pieces relative to all complete and broken pieces, can then be calculated. It is important not to include distal or medial fragments in the calculation. A single flake can break into many fragments, but there will be only one proximal end.

Postdepositional artifact damage can significantly alter an assemblage in ways that resemble human behavioral modifications. For example, edge damage such as that described here can be difficult to differentiate from macroscopic use wear and it can also be easily mistaken for retouch. This is especially true in the case of notched and denticulate tool types. If you are analyzing an assemblage where such processes may have been operating, you should assign only clear cases to these tool types. Other types, especially the abrupt and alternating types (type 48), are probably best interpreted as reflecting disturbance rather than human behavior.

Obviously the identification of damage can be subjective and is an ambiguous indicator of postdepositional disturbance. Cultural activities can also cause damage. For example, use of an artifact results in both microscopic and macroscopic edge damage, ridges can suffer from abrasion because of hafting, and flakes and tools are broken during both production and use. Trampling can also cause edge damage and artifact breakage and can result in the production of pseudo-tools because the damage can resemble deliberate retouch (McBrearty et al. 1998). Even if a significant degree of damage and breakage is present in an assemblage, other aspects of the assemblage and the site geology should be examined to confirm that geological disturbance was the primary cause.

SIZE DISTRIBUTIONS

During the process of flintknapping a wide range of object sizes are produced, from large flakes, tools, and cores, through smaller retouch flakes, down to microscopic particles. As a result of a number of quantitative replicative experiments, we now have some understanding of the expected distribution of flake size in an assemblage: smaller sizes are represented in increasing frequency. Although the upper size range may vary, the general shape of the distribution seems to hold true despite differing technologies or differing degrees of core reduction. With this type of distribution, we would expect to find many more small flakes than large ones.

Natural processes, especially water action, may differentially remove small flakes from an assemblage. As stream flow increases (or as the slope gradient increases in slopewash), the water is capable of transporting increasingly heavy sediment loads. This means that increasingly larger flakes will be removed and redeposited downstream as the flow eventually diminishes. Thus if a lithic assemblage is composed of mostly larger pieces, it is quite likely that water action was responsible for the size distribution and transported smaller, lighter objects away from the site (Schick 1986).

ARTIFACT ORIENTATIONS

Relatively new to archaeological taphonomic studies, but well known in geological research, are analyses based on the distribution of both the horizontal (declination) and vertical (inclination) orientations of artifacts. Usually artifacts that fall to the ground will orient themselves horizontally in a random pattern and vertically in alignment with the existing surface. However, various natural agencies, primarily water action and mass wasting (soil movement), will alter these patterns and leave telltale signatures that they have affected the lithic assemblage (Kluskens 1995, Rick 1976).

Streams and slopewash have a pronounced effect on horizontal and vertical artifact orientations. As water flows past elongated artifacts they will tend to align themselves either parallel to the flow of water (as a way of decreasing their resistance to the flow) or, when the flow is strong, perpendicular to it (which makes it easier for them to roll along the streambed). Thus a uni- or bimodal distribution of artifact declinations at angles parallel and perpendicular to the flow will indicate at least some water action. The inclination of the artifacts is not affected as much, although artifacts subjected to water action will tend to dip slightly down in their upstream (or upslope) angle relative to the natural gradient. This slight dipping is called imbrication.

One of the more common mass movements in periglacial environments is solifluction, which occurs as sediments slide down a slope. With solifluction, elongated artifacts tend to be realigned parallel to the flow, especially those within the soliflucted sediment (as opposed to those lying on the surface). Likewise, solifluction tends to dip down, or imbricate, the upslope end of artifacts up to 30–55 degrees from the slope angle, although if there is significant churning of sediments, inclination angles may be dispersed widely.

A complex folding or churning of the sediments often characterizes solifluction and related processes such as debris flow. This will result in dispersed inclination distributions as the artifacts lose their original tendency to follow the slope.

By comparing the declination and inclination of artifacts with natural stones in the matrix, it is possible to see if they show different orientations. The more the artifacts match the surrounding geological matrix in orientations and size, the more likely it is that the artifacts were deposited with the sediments and not independently by humans or that they were affected by the same postdepositional processes as the surrounding sediments.

By looking at orientations within levels at a site, it is possible to determine the extent and nature of geological disturbance. If artifacts show a patterned horizontal orientation, they were likely affected by geological processes because random human discard would not result in consistent declinations. In contrast, the lack of clear patterning of vertical inclination angles (along the slope) would indicate that something churned up the sediment and the artifacts within it. To see examples of declination and inclination and how they are represented visually in radar graphs, choose the **Analysis/Artifact Orientations** option, and click on the **Declination** and **Inclination** tabs.

SITE TAPHONOMY AT COMBE-CAPELLE

The study of site formation was a major focus of our work at Combe-Capelle. We realized from the outset that the probability of some degree of postdepositional disturbance was high because the site was located on a hill slope. We were interested in determining the degree to which the site had been disturbed.

To assess site taphonomy we drew on several lines of evidence: geological studies, the density of small finds, the analysis of artifact edge damage, and the analysis of artifact orientations. We calculated and compared artifact densities across the site using material recovered during wet screening of each bucket, and we recorded orientations by measuring the ends of elongated artifacts over 3 cm in size. We used the data to calculate the declination and inclination for each geological level in order to look at the overall pattern of artifact orientations.

Suggested Readings

Dibble et al. 1997; Schick 1986; Schiffer 1972, 1987; Stein 1987; Villa and Courtin 1983; Wood and Johnson 1978

EXERCISE 20.1

Site Taphonomy

Load the real Combe-Capelle data, and go to the **Analysis/Artifact Orientations** screen. For the following questions, we will look at level I-2A.

1. Calculate the orientations for level I-2A and graph the results. Now go back to the graphs on the **Declination** and **Inclination** tabs and compare your graphs with these. Do the inclinations follow the slope of the hill? Do the declinations appear random, or do they also seem to follow the slope? What does this tell you about the depositional history of this level?

2. Another way to evaluate taphonomy is to look at edge-damaged pieces. Go to the **Statistics, Tables, and Graphs** screen and click on the **Analyze Field** tab. Analyze edge damage by level by using bar charts with percentage data. Do the assemblages show a lot of edge damage?

3. Choose **Creating Type Lists** and create a type list for all levels for your virtual project and create a cumulative graph. Do you have a high percentage of types 48 and 49 in your assemblage (look in the type spreadsheet and the cumulative graph)?

Writing a Site Report

21

After you have completed your excavation and analysis comes the most important part of archaeological fieldwork: writing the report. It is essential that you publish the results of your fieldwork in a timely manner to make the data available to other researchers.

The site report should be written clearly and should describe the research design, the field and analysis methods, the results of your fieldwork and analysis, and your interpretations of the data. Data should be incorporated in all discussions within the body of the site report and should be included in tables and graphs within the report to support the inferences you make about the site. Data can also be included within an appendix or on a computer disk so that others interested in your results can either independently check the data or expand upon your research.

As the final exercise for your virtual project, you are to write a report on the results of your excavations at Combe-Capelle.

The following guidelines include basic information that should be included in any site report:

- *Research design.* Summarize the research design, specifically the research questions you addressed with the data collected during excavation.

- *Background research.* Summarize what was known about the site, how it ties into regional prehistory (in this case, the European Middle Paleolithic), and major issues dealing with your specific site or time period.

- *Field and analysis methods.* Provide a general description of how you excavated and analyzed the material. Include a description of your excavation units, the tools you used, and methods for proveniencing and screening. Define the attributes you used in your lithic analysis.

- *Results of fieldwork.* Describe what you found during excavation. Discuss the stratigraphy and taphonomic processes operating on the site and any other factors that might influence the interpretation of these results. Also include in this section a discussion of things that you planned to do but could not do.

- *Results of analysis.* Describe what you found during the analysis of the artifacts from the site. The results of your analysis will often be presented using tables and graphs that will make the data more understandable.

- *Synthesis and interpretations of the results.* This is the "meat" of the site report. In this section you bring together all of the data you obtained during fieldwork and analysis, and seek to answer your research questions and draw inferences about what happened at the site. The inferences should be based on the data you obtained and will sometimes be different from what you expected. That is the nature of archaeological research. Remember that the archaeological record is incomplete; therefore, the inferences you make based on the excavation of a site may change as other sites are investigated and more data become available.

As part of the final report for your virtual project, include a final budget by printing out your budget screen. If you have gone over budget you need to explain why in the final report.

References

Barker, P. 1993. *Techniques of archaeological excavation.* New York: Universe Books.

Binford, L. 1964. A consideration of archaeological research design. *American Antiquity* 29:425–441.

———. 1973. Interassemblage variability: The Mousterian and the functional argument. In *The explanation of culture change,* edited by C. Renfrew, pp. 227–254. London: Duckworth.

Binford, L., and S. Binford. 1966. A preliminary analysis of functional variability in the Mousterian of Levallois facies. *American Anthropologist* 68:238–295.

Bordaz, J. 1970. *Tools of the old and new stone age.* New York: Natural History Press.

Bordes, F. 1961a. Mousterian cultures in France. *Science* 134:803–810.

———. 1961b. *Typologie du Paléolithique Ancien et Moyen.* Paris: Centre National de la Recherche Scientifique.

———. 1972. *A tale of two caves.* New York: Harper and Row.

———. 1973. On the chronology and contemporaneity of different Paleolithic cultures in France. In *The explanation of culture change,* edited by C. Renfrew, pp. 217–226. London: Duckworth.

Bourgon, M. 1957. *Les industries mousteriennes et pré-mousteriennes du Périgord.* Archives de l'Institut de Paleontologie Humaine Memoire 27. Paris: Masson.

Chase, P. G., and H. L. Dibble. 1987. Middle Paleolithic symbolism: A review of current evidence and interpretations. *Journal of Anthropological Archaeology* 6:263–296.

Debénath, A., and H. L. Dibble. 1994. *The handbook of Paleolithic typology.* Vol. 1, *The Lower and Middle Paleolithic of Europe.* Philadelphia: University Museum Press.

Dibble, H. L. 1987. Measurement of artifact provenience with an electronic theodolite. *Journal of Field Archaeology* 14:249–254.

———. 1995. Middle Paleolithic scraper reduction: Background, clarification, and review of evidence to data. *Journal of Archaeological Method and Theory* 2(4):299–368.

———. 1997. Platform variability and flake morphology: A comparison of experimental and archaeological data and implications for interpreting prehistoric lithic technological strategies. *Lithic Technology* 22(2):150–170.

Dibble, H. L., P. G. Chase, S. McPherron, and A. Tuffreau. 1997. Testing the reality of a "living floor" with archaeological data. *American Antiquity* 62(4):629–651.

Dibble, H. L., and M. Lenoir, eds. 1995. *The Middle Paleolithic site of Combe-Capelle Bas (France).* Philadelphia: University Museum Press.

Dibble, H. L., and S. McPherron. 1989. On the computerization of archaeological projects. *Journal of Field Archaeology* 15(4):431–440.

———. 1996. *Combe-Capelle on CD-ROM: A multimedia companion to* The Middle Paleolithic site of Combe-Capelle Bas (France). Philadelphia: University Museum Press.

———. 1997. The making of *Combe-Capelle on CD-ROM. Journal of Field Archaeology* 24(1):59–66.

Dibble, H. L., and P. Mellars, eds. 1992. *The Middle Paleolithic: Adaptation, behavior, and variability.* Philadelphia: University Museum Press.

Drucker, P. 1972. *Stratigraphy in archaeology: An introduction.* New York: Addison-Wesley.

Fish, P. 1978. Consistency in archaeological measurement and classification: A pilot study. *American Antiquity* 43(1):86–89.

Gargett, R. H. 1989. Grave shortcomings: The evidence for Neandertal burial. *Current Anthropology* 30:157–190.

Gladfelter, B. G. 1981. Developments and directions in geoarchaeology. In *Advances in archaeological method and theory,* edited by M. B. Schiffer, pp. 343–364. New York: Academic Press.

Harris, E. C. 1975. The stratigraphic sequence: A question of time. *World Archaeology* 7:109–121.

———. 1989. *Principles of archaeological stratigraphy.* London: Academic Press.

Hassan, F. 1978. Sediments in archaeology: Methods and implications for paleoenvironmental and cultural analysis. *Journal of Field Archaeology* 5:197–213.

Hayden, B. 1993. *Archaeology: The science of once and future things.* New York: W. H. Freeman.

Hester, T. R., H. J. Shafer, and K. L. Feder. 1997. *Field methods in archaeology.* Mountain View, Calif.: Mayfield.

Joukowsky, M. E. 1980. *A complete manual of field archaeology.* Englewood Cliffs, N. J.: Prentice-Hall.

Kluskens, S. L. 1995. Archaeological taphonomy of Combe-Capelle Bas from artifact orientation and density analysis. In *The Middle Paleolithic site of Combe-Capelle Bas (France),* edited by H. L. Dibble and M. Lenoir, pp. 199–243. Philadelphia: University Museum Press.

Laville, H., J.-P. Rigaud, and J. R. Sackett. 1980. *Rock shelters of the Perigord: Geological stratigraphy and archaeological succession.* New York: Academic Press.

McBrearty, S., L. Bishop, T. Plummer, R. Dewar, and N. J. Conard. 1998. Tools underfoot: Human trampling as an agent of lithic artifact edge modification. *American Antiquity* 63:108–129.

Mellars, P. 1965. Sequence and development of the Mousterian traditions in southwestern France. *Nature* 205: 626–627.

——. 1969. The chronology of Mousterian industries in the Perigord region. *Proceedings of the Prehistoric Society* 35:134–171.

——. 1996. *The Neanderthal legacy: An archaeological perspective from western Europe.* Princeton: Princeton University Press.

Rick, J. W. 1976. Downslope movement and archaeological intrasite spatial analysis. *American Antiquity* 41: 133–144.

Rolland, N., and H. L. Dibble. 1990. A new synthesis of Middle Paleolithic assemblage variability. *American Antiquity* 55(3):480–499.

Schick, K. 1986. *Stone Age sites in the making: Experiments in the formation and transformation of archaeological occurrences.* British Archaeological Reports International Series 319, Oxford.

Schiffer, M. B. 1972. Archaeological context and systemic context. *American Antiquity* 37:156–165.

——. 1983. Toward the identification of formation processes. *American Antiquity* 48:675–706.

——. 1985. Is there a "Pompeii Premise" in archaeology? *Journal of Anthropological Research* 41:18–41.

——. 1987. *Formation processes of the archaeological record.* Albuquerque: University of New Mexico Press.

Sharer, R. J., and W. Ashmore. 1993. *Archaeology: Discovering our past.* Mountain View, Calif.: Mayfield.

Stein, J. K. 1987. Deposits for archaeologists. In *Advances in archaeological method and theory.* Vol. 11, edited by M. B. Schiffer, pp. 337–395. New York: Academic Press.

Stringer, C., and C. Gamble. 1993. *In search of the Neanderthals: Solving the puzzle of human origins.* London: Thames and Hudson.

Struever, S. 1971. Comments on archaeological data requirements and research designs. *American Antiquity* 36:9–19.

Sullivan, A., and K. Rozen. 1985. Debitage analysis and archaeological interpretation. *American Antiquity* 50: 755–779.

Thomas, D. H. 1995. *Archaeology.* New York: Holt, Rinehart and Winston.

Trinkaus, E., and P. Shipman. 1993. *The Neandertals: Changing the image of mankind.* New York: Alfred Knopf.

Villa, P., and J. Courtin. 1983. The interpretation of stratified sites: A view from underground. *Journal of Archaeological Science* 10:267–281.

Whittaker, J. 1994. *Flintknapping: Making and understanding stone tools.* Austin: University of Texas Press.

Wood, R., and D. L. Johnson. 1978. A survey of disturbance processes in site formation. In *Advances in archaeological method and theory.* Vol. 1, edited by M. B. Schiffer, pp. 315–381. New York: Academic Press.

Index